Walk

Your

Talk

Your 4-week programme to take action now and change your life

Walk Your Talk

Sunday Times bestselling author
Theresa Cheung

WALK YOUR TALK
Theresa Cheung

This edition first published in the UK and USA in 2025 by
Watkins, an imprint of Watkins Media Limited
Unit 11, Shepperton House,
89-93 Shepperton Road,
London
N1 3DF

enquiries@watkinspublishing.com

1 3 5 7 9 10 8 6 4 2

Printed and bound in CPI Group (UK), Ltd. Croydon, CR0 4YY

A CIP record for this book is available from the British Library

ISBN: 978-1-78678-975-4 (paperback)
ISBN: 978-1-78678-976-1 (ebook)

www.watkinspublishing.com

The manufacturer's authorised representative in the EU for product safety is
eucomply OÜ - Pärnu mnt 139b-14, 11317 Tallinn, Estonia,
hello@eucompliancepartner.com,www.eucompliancepartner.com

*"Don't explain your philosophy,
embody it."*

Epictetus

CONTENTS

PREFACE: SO, WHAT DO YOU DO?

How many times have you been asked, "So, what do you do?" in your life?

I'm guessing you've lost count.

Whether it arises in job interviews, networking events, at parties or at family gatherings, it's the inescapable looming question. Sometimes you may find it easier to answer than at others, but I'm also guessing every time you've been asked it, you've sighed a little inside. Not just because the question is so darn predictable, but because it is *the* question. You know you will be instantly defined and caged in by your answer.

Walk Your Talk will radically reinvent your response to that dreaded question. You will know exactly how to impress on both yourself and others that your current role, situation, title or job description doesn't identify or define you. Your life is so much bigger and greater than that.

Whether or not you choose to share any further details about yourself when you're next asked the question, you'll make it clear from the outset that you're busy living life and doing it in the greatest way possible – your way, regardless of what anyone else thinks, feels or expects of you.

So, if you want to start living life your way and feel inspired and empowered by every step you take, don't hesitate. This book is here to liberate you not just from the dreaded "So, what do you do?" question, but from all those other pesky limitations that have previously stopped you in your tracks.

Read on. It's your time to begin the adventure and take life-changing action, right now.

INTRODUCTION: SHOW, DON'T TELL

"What we do now echoes in eternity."

Marcus Aurelius, *Meditations*

Notice the choice of words in the famous quote above: it's not what you think or what you feel, but what you do that sets you up for greatness. And not only that, what you do affects your present, your future, other people and what you're remembered for.

Attributed to the ancient Roman philosopher Marcus Aurelius, this quote became even more iconic when it was spoken by the character of Maximus, played by actor Russell Crowe, in *Gladiator*, a movie directed by Ridley Scott (2000). Through the course of his story, Maximus shows himself to be a great leader and, more importantly, a truly great man. When he utters that memorable line, it has the desired effect of motivating and strengthening his soldiers. They follow him not because they must, but because they want to.

I'm not suggesting in any way here that the battlefield is a place to prove your worth, but I'm sharing this quote at the very beginning of the book because the character of Maximus embodies the qualities of true greatness – qualities we all aspire to live by. These qualities include unwavering integrity, steadfast determination, powerful discipline, outstanding courage and, most admirable of all, the powerful ability to lead by example.

Maximus's story is impactful because his life is his message and his legacy. If you haven't seen the movie, you're missing out, as it's harrowing at times but mighty empowering. Maximus is a Roman general who is betrayed and reduced to slavery. He becomes a gladiator and rises through the ranks, determined to avenge the murder of his family and to fight injustice.

His character inspires in others a desire to make greatness their only story. He shows us how a great life is defined not so much by achievements or whether you succeed or fail, or by your current job title or role, but by your ability to live the values you espouse. It's about the integrity of your actions. It is about walking your talk.

The Importance of Your Daily Actions

The problem is that many of us don't pay nearly enough attention to our daily actions. We typically look to the transformative power of thoughts and feelings when we seek to change our lives for the better. We may seek out meditation, talking therapies, retreats, manifesting, mindfulness courses and so on. We may even repeat affirmations and get fixated by the "believe it before you see it" manifesting mantra that's so prevalent right now in the self-help and personal growth movement – according to which you've truly got to believe you're worthy first. Easier said than done, when life sucks.

To some extent, self-reflection can be helpful, as self-knowledge is the beginning of all wisdom, and choosing healthy thoughts can help create a much-needed inner shift. But it's pointless to practise self-awareness and positive thinking without taking action to validate this. That only leads to weakness and uncertainty, not strength and determination.

In recent years, there has been a lot of emphasis in the self-help industry on the life-changing power of belief. The advice in manifesting is to visualize positivity for yourself constantly, as everything in the universe is energy – including your thoughts – the theory being that like energy seeks like energy. In other words, if you think, believe and feel positive, that's what you'll attract energetically.

However, if you've ever tried positive thinking and it just hasn't worked out for you, you could find that switching your focus to your daily actions holds the answer to making all those good intentions materialize. A tangible common-sense starting point, the place to begin when you want to change your life isn't always with a vision board or by looking in the mirror – it's with your daily actions. Your actions, whether you feel like doing them at the time or not, are the answer. But not mindless actions. Knowing which specific daily actions are the most empowering power moves for you is the life-changing secret this book will share with you.

That's why this book is your pre-manifesting essential. It can prepare you to become a manifester when you don't feel you are one or if, no matter how hard you try to be upbeat, your thoughts keep naturally drifting downstream. In fact, by the time that you complete the action-packed programme shared in the pages that follow, you may even find that you're already manifesting a more fulfilling life.

Choose your daily actions wisely first. Without that solid action-focused foundation firmly in place, your life simply isn't going to change for the better, no matter how much willpower you put into your visualizations, affirmations and intentions.

The Greek philosopher Aristotle was spot-on when he stated, "We are what we repeatedly do." Your daily actions, rather than your thoughts and feelings, truly are what define and constantly redefine you. What you do – not what you dream about or wish to do with your one precious life – is how happiness is achieved and, how your life is measured.

If you're looking to connect to your inner Maximus – the true potential for outstanding integrity and greatness within you – *Walk Your Talk* is the common-sense breakthrough and action-coach programme you may have been waiting your whole life for.

Be Like the Tortoise

Reading and acting on the advice in this book is the first and most important step to creating positive and lasting change in your life, setting you on your true path to greatness.

Commit to it. But don't just read it out of curiosity and put the recommendations on your "to do" list. Scrap the "to" and put it on your "do now" list. And then do it regardless of what you think and feel, because there is never a perfect time. And to maximize your chances of success, do it tortoise-style, like the winner of the race in Aesop's fable "The Tortoise and the Hare".

Change rarely happens overnight. It is the result of small, steady and persistent daily steps or actions you take in a positive direction. Nothing illustrates this better than Edison and his famous light bulb experiments. When a reporter asked inventor Thomas Edison how it felt to fail 1,000 times before he invented the light bulb, Edison famously replied: "I didn't fail 1,000 times. The light bulb was an invention with 1,000 steps." Each one of those 999 missteps took as much patience, time and dedication as the final successful step.

In other words, it doesn't matter how slow and steady you go, nor how many times you stumble and fall; as long as you don't stop you'll fail upwards. Any time you're tempted to act like the competitive hare in the fable, you seriously risk burnout. Chances are you're only eager to push forward because you want to impress others with your victory lap. You want them to see you winning, even though – and here's a life hack for you – most people really don't care what you're doing or whether you're succeeding or not.

They're probably far too busy wondering what others think of them to worry about what you're up to! Escape that addiction to validation from others and handing your power over to them in the process. Focus on your own goals and your own dreams and take your power back with your daily actions. Jump off the "please applaud and like me" treadmill now and concentrate fully on impressing yourself. Focus on your own path and doing the best you can. Above all, remember that every small step you take, even if it doesn't work out or proves to be a disaster, is about you learning and growing, and evolution is what gives your life its meaning and purpose. So even when you mess up, you're still living the meaning and purpose of your life your way.

Wait for It . . .

If given the choice, chances are most of us would take an instant financial windfall over compound interest. But any clued-up investor will tell you that compound interest earns you more income in the long run. Similarly, the messaging of today's "live in the moment" culture hinders our ability to invest in ourselves for the long term.

Consider a fascinating study conducted in the 1970s, led by psychologist and Stanford professor Walter Mischel, known as the Stanford Marshmallow experiment. In the study, a group of 50 children were offered a choice between one reward now or two rewards if they waited for a period of time. A researcher left each child in a room with a single marshmallow for about 15 minutes and then returned. If the child didn't eat the marshmallow, the reward was another marshmallow. Follow-up studies revealed that the children who were able to wait longer – in other words, delay their gratification – tended to have better life outcomes.[1]

The results of the study have been challenged over the years, and there is doubt about whether it showcases the rewards of willpower or not, given that children were the participants. But it does strongly indicate that focusing on long- rather than short-term gain is the smarter life choice.

The point is that if you want your life to transform in a positive way, you don't need to start with dramatic change. Despite what you may have been told, this is rarely the solution. You need to start with the small things you repeatedly and consistently do, knowing that they're all steps toward your end goal. True change is the compound result of a series of small daily actions, which in this book we'll call your daily power moves.

From now on, whether you feel the time is right or not, I'd like you to start taking these small practical steps every single day to keep yourself steadily moving forward in the right direction. You need to take your own sweet time and invest in yourself – like the tortoise, not the hare.

There are some major life changes, such as moving house, divorce, a change of career, changing country of residence and so on, but these don't always improve your life in the long term. They create short-term opportunities to progress, but if you truly want to see long-term positive change, you need, like Dorothy at the end of *The Wizard of Oz*, to look much closer to home. You need to look at what you repeatedly do every single day.

To sum up:

- How you live your life is your message, your legacy.
- You simply can't control what other people think about you, so let go of any need to control them. Focus instead on what you can control – which is your daily actions.
- You are what you consistently do every day, not what you think, feel, say, hope, visualize or affirm.
- Your daily actions – the small things you repeatedly do – are both the cause and the effect of motivation. They are the secret to living an empowered life both today and tomorrow. They are your forever power moves.

Your Power Moves

Research backs up the life-changing power of doing, and indicates that your daily actions create your present and dramatically increase your chances of success both personally and professionally.[2] Studies have shown that establishing and sticking to routines regardless can dramatically enhance performance when willpower is low.[3]

Studies also prove that it's not just your thoughts that shape your brain and therefore your life; your daily actions also shape your brain and life.[4,5] If you've ever felt your mood lift after going for a brisk walk, you'll instinctively know the truth of this science. We might have got it all wrong: change starts with the actions we repeatedly take, rather than what we think.

In addition, research shows that the predictability of performing certain daily actions that we know are life-enhancing can decrease anxiety and create a feeling of inner calm.[6,7] This matters greatly too, because other studies show that anxiety is the single biggest reason for poor decision-making in life.[8]

In short, the more power moves there are to add structure and direction to your day, the more in control of your life you'll become and the happier you'll feel. And the calmer you are, the better life choices you'll make, dramatically increasing your chances of success. And if you're wondering what these power moves are, or which specific actions you can do each day that are the most life-enhancing, all will be revealed in your upcoming Four-Week Action Plan.

Do and Understand the Doing

In the immortal words attributed to the Chinese philosopher Confucius: "What I hear I forget. What I see I remember. What I do I understand."

You need not only to read and understand but *do* the specific power moves in this book, because if you don't do them what you'll have is knowledge, but no understanding gained from direct personal experience. Knowledge is not your teacher; experiencing something and the understanding that the experience gives you are.

As soon as you begin the programme in this book, you'll be encouraged to transform many of your established daily routines into a series of power moves. These small, practical changes will create an immediate shift and build momentum in your here and now, while at the same time forming a remarkable investment in your future well-being.

Stick with your power moves programme for at least one month and your investment in yourself will begin to pay off. You will start to feel stronger physically, mentally and emotionally. Stick with it for one year and your life will be completely transformed.

Willpower Alone isn't Enough

Sorry to break it to you, but willpower alone can't change your life, despite what you may hear about the power of manifesting. Yes, willpower matters – and in some cases it can move mountains – but this doesn't mean it's always the best starting point, especially if being a glass-half-full person isn't your default setting. The best starting point for personal growth is changing your daily actions and understanding why you're changing them: because you want to feel better about yourself and your life. The knowing why you are doing something is the key motivator here. If you don't know why you are doing something, you won't be motivated to do it. But when you are made aware of the "why", your brain will have no choice but to follow where your actions take you, and sooner or later your willpower, if it wasn't strong before, will arise naturally. Your mind follows your body as much as your body follows your mind.

Regardless of whether you're a "just say yes" or a "just say no" kind of person, the optimum launch pad for positive change is your own body power. And by that, I don't mean going to the gym. I mean doing certain things every day that don't require much willpower at all, but which will help you become the great and inspiring person you know you can be – that rare person whose daily actions match their words.

If you've tried and failed to create change through positive thinking, vision boards, visualizations and affirmations – finding your progress to be one step forward, ten steps back – then know that you have in your hands a book that is finally going to make the difference. It will help you feel better within a matter of weeks and at the same time initiate lasting change. It's also easy to do everything in it and to keep on doing it, and best of all there isn't an affirmation or any mystical mumbo jumbo in sight!

Your power move programme won't make you feel like a failure if your life doesn't suddenly change. It reminds you repeatedly that you're investing in yourself now for the long term. It's based entirely on research into successful and sustained behaviour changes and it focuses on the power of small actions taken daily and consistently.

It also reminds you that a great life isn't something out there waiting for you on the horizon. A great life is to be found in every step you take, every single day, right here, right now. It's the steady but progressive way of the tortoise. The tortoise may be slow but it wins that race. Better still, the tortoise savours the journey; it gets to smell the roses along the way to its destination!

I Do, I Do, I Do

The effectiveness of the suggested daily actions – or power moves – lies in their daily and consistent repetition.[9] There's no point in doing this programme every now and again; you need to do the power moves daily for at least a month. This shouldn't be a problem, because all the power moves take just a moment or so to perform, have the backing of research and will involve actions – simple things you can repeatedly do.

A necessary reminder: the emphasis throughout is on the power of "I do", not "I think", or "I feel", or "I believe", because just as we trust people in life by their actions, not their words, you need to prove to yourself, others and the world that you're the real deal. You are a role model, a person of their word, someone worth investing time and energy in. You don't delay or dither in the way suggested by the all too commonly heard phrases coming up below; you act here and now.

I'll Get Back to You

Do any of the following sound familiar?

- "I'll get back to you later this week." (*The week passes without an update.*)
- "Sure, I'll let you know shortly." (*"Shortly" becomes indefinitely.*)
- "Yes, we'll definitely keep in touch." (*You do. They don't.*)

It's frustrating and disempowering, isn't it, when you trust someone to be true to their word, but their actions speak the total opposite?

Be honest now. In your own life, have you ever promised and not delivered? How many times have you said you would do something and then didn't?

In most cases, both when other people let you down and when you let yourself down through promises made and not kept, this wasn't the original intention. When the promise is made it's often made in earnest, but then life gets in the way, and it's forgotten.

It might be impossible to follow through 100 per cent on your word every time, but it is possible to make sure from now on that your words mean something both to yourself and others. Because the way you interact with other people mirrors the way you interact with yourself. If you let others down, or don't follow through, or at the very least update, chances are you'll constantly be letting yourself down, too, or not following through on your own intentions. And that is not a good thing. It stops right here, in this present moment.

From Now On

The modern world increasingly seems to be one in which "promises made, promises not kept" has become the order of the day. It can be hard to know when someone is speaking the truth, especially in the online world where alternative facts and spin proliferate. The globally popular TV show *The Traitors* – where the ability to deceive is the only path to victory – is a great way to witness people saying what they don't mean, words not matching actions and the strategies used to deceive. But the ability to make false promises should never be glamorized. Despite the illusion of success and so-called "cleverness", empty words are a sure-fire recipe for an empty life. Besides this, the original meaning of the Sanskrit term "karma" is "action" or "deed"; and whether or not we believe in the spiritual concept of karma, the truth is that our actions have a habit of coming back to bite us in some shape or form.

I'm assuming that you're reading this book because you want to feel great about your life. So, make an unbreakable promise to yourself now to incorporate the recommended power moves in this book into your daily life for a minimum of four weeks. And endeavour to keep that promise, come what may. It's very important that from now on no more promises are made to yourself and others and not kept.

Let this be a new beginning.

And while you're making a fresh start, now is the ideal time to stop oversharing, too. Lay off all that sharing and confiding. Leave all the talking and explaining to others. Go dark for a while as you sort out yourself and your life.

This book has called your name loud and clear.

You need to show, not tell, yourself, others and the world what you are really made of.

Who am I?

You might very well be wondering what qualifies me to take this action-orientated stand and write this book. I've been a bestselling writer, teacher and speaker for decades in the spirituality, personal growth and development movement. People often look at my extensive output and the longevity of it and ask me how on earth I do it. The answer is simple. I practise what I preach, and I have learned the hard way how important – crucial – it is to focus more on doing than on thinking and, above all, to follow through.

For many years, I've thought, dreamed, written and talked about mainstreaming the advice I offer in my books. The written word is a great way to get your message across, but to reach a wider global audience I knew deep down I would have to try other ways. It was always a vague idea out there on the horizon. I always found excuses not to put it into action and stuck with writing book after book. I stayed in my comfort zone, hiding safely behind my computer and bashing away at the keyboard.

But then, about five years ago, when I started to research, write about and truly live the power moves I'll share in this book, my life changed dramatically because I moved from being passive to active, from talk to walk. Within weeks I let go of fear and hesitation and launched my first podcast, *White Shores*. I reached out to some of the world's leading personal and spiritual growth scientists, psychologists, practitioners and thought leaders. Some said no but some said yes, and even though I had no experience as an interviewer I went for it.

White Shores wasn't an overnight success, but the downloads were in their hundreds and that was highly encouraging. Slow and steady like the tortoise, I carried on podcasting, one episode at a time. Today, I'm proud to say *White Shores* ranks in the top podcasts globally and I have a waiting list of amazing people wanting to appear on it and thousands of enthusiastic listeners. Best of all, I feel alive every time I record and release an episode. I hope every episode informs, inspires and enlightens my listeners. *White Shores* is my creation. My message to the world. It is something I'm very proud to say I repeatedly do.

All my life, I have worked with passion, discipline and determination toward my goals. This doesn't mean I haven't had failures; trust me, I've had more than my fair share of them. But I have learned to use those inevitable setbacks as teachers and course-correctors. I've also learned again the hard way to trust people by their actions rather than their words.

Ten years ago, I got caught up with a group of people who said all the right things as far as the progression of my career was concerned. It was intoxicating to spend time doing endless vision boards with them and attending countless meetings. But over the course of a few months, I discovered the perils of relying on words and blindly trusting those who flatter, overpromise and under-deliver. My personal and professional life suffered greatly, and it took me several years to get back on track.

I won't bore you with the details, because I want this book to be all about you and not me, but I want you to know from the outset that even though I didn't realize it at the time, the seeds of this book were being sown many years ago. All my life experience is in this book. It's a book I wish I'd read decades ago, because if I had, I would have had a head start, known how to spot red flags and seen how vital it is to trust others according to their deeds and not their eloquence. And how the person I most needed to keep my promises to was myself. How life-enhancing it is not just to think, hope, dream, advise, discuss and debate, but to get out there, face my fears, and just do.

If you decide to follow me on social media after reading this book, I hope you'll see me time and time again putting myself right outside my comfort zone, challenging myself, falling, getting up and learning and growing wiser as I do. Walking my talk and living my life as the action-adventure message it should be. I enjoy showing my loved ones and family, as well as my publishers, readers and podcast listeners, that I'm not trapped inside my own head. I'm getting out there and living my message, rather than simply writing or talking or theorizing about it.

I hope that after reading this book, you'll have everything you need in place to break free from the tyranny of affirmations and become the action hero of your own life, too.

Stepping Out

In the pages that follow, you'll find a series of 22 simple daily actions – power moves – that will set you up for greatness if you incorporate them into your routine. They're tried-and-tested things you can immediately start doing today. Some will seem radical and new, while others may seem like recycled common sense, but whatever your reaction, it's important that you start doing them and do them repeatedly, for the simple reason that they're your direct path to personal greatness.

Each power move is presented in the same way for ease and clarity.

First, the action is introduced, along with the reason you're being asked to do it, some background explanation and a brief, generic case history. Don't be tempted to skim read this section, as you will need to understand why you're being asked to do something before you start doing it. It's another important reminder that your actions should always be living embodiments of who you truly are. They should also not be performed mindlessly but done with intention and understanding, personalized as much as possible. You're living out your authentic self, getting out of your head and into your body and your life.

Second, the most effective ways to incorporate the power move into your daily routine are outlined. Simple!

Timing is Everything

Staying true to our winning tortoise formula, the 22 power moves will be introduced slowly and carefully, one step at a time over a period of four weeks, with Week One introducing you to eight power moves. Week Two will add a further four, Week Three will add nine more to your repertoire and Week Four crescendos with the final master power move, which should only be tackled when the other 21 are all incorporated. Each day, you'll be asked to add one or two more power moves to your repertoire, building momentum and spiralling onward and upward as you go. You're strongly advised to stick to the formula and to add at least one more power move each day into your daily routine so that when you enter Week Four, you'll have all 22 power moves in place. In short,

- Week One will focus on your morning motivation.
- Week Two empowers your evenings.
- Week Three walks you through your day with calm purpose.
- Week Four encompasses everything.

By the end of the fourth week, you should have all 22 power moves marching in lockstep and taking you in the right direction. At some point around the Week Four mark, you'll start feeling the benefits of the power moves from Week One, if you're repeating them daily and consistently. This is because four weeks is how long it typically takes before an action will start to become habitual – meaning it happens with no questions asked and you don't have to think very much about just doing it.[10] It's simply something you routinely do because you know it's good for you and you can feel the benefits, like brushing your teeth.

At the five or six-week mark, you'll keenly feel the benefits of the Week Two power moves, alongside those of Week One. Around the seven or eight-week mark, those Week Three power moves kick right in, and then in nine or ten weeks the spotlight will be completely on you. You'll be swiftly becoming the star and action hero of your own life.

After that don't stop, just keep on going. Your daily actions – empowered by the 22 power moves you keep repeating – will have begun to rewire your brain and body, transforming you into a person of great integrity, discipline and action. A person you and others can wholeheartedly trust and passionately admire.

Potential Pitfalls

Yes, you can change your life for the better if you follow through with these 22 daily actions and stick with doing them for at least a month or two, and ideally for the rest of your life. But as you go boldly forward you need to be aware of the trapdoors and landmines that you're most likely to come across along the way.

I'm going to describe the most likely ones here so that you can prepare for them before you start. After all, forewarned is forearmed . . .

Overthinking

At some point you might be tempted to think it's all too good to be true. This can't be for real. Your life needs a lot more than a few simple actions to mark you out for success. At the same time, you may start thinking about your problems again and the mountains you need to climb to overcome them. You feel tempted to go back to the drawing or vision board and make new self-help plans.

See what's happening here? Acting is being replaced by

overthinking. It may feel productive to revise your plans constantly – and to worry excessively about them – but what you're doing is zoning in on what you can't control in your life. The solution is not more worrying. I hate to break it to you but while worrying may feel like hard work, it's not actually accomplishing anything. It achieves precisely nothing. You need to focus on what you can control, which are your daily actions. You need to get out of your thoughts and back into your body and your daily life. Let go of what you can't control, most especially the opinions of others, and direct the wasted energy you've been sending out there to others toward yourself instead. Stick with your daily action plan. Think less. Do more.

Unrealistic expectations
Unrealistic expectations are another action stopper. Your expectation for change is so high that you inevitably fail to impress yourself when it doesn't happen right away. This can cause despondency when you don't immediately see progress or feel any different, leading to a "what's the point" outlook.

The antidote is once again to remind yourself of the small, steady steps that the tortoise took toward the winning post in Aesop's fable. Each one of those steps may have felt futile at the time – as if they had no purpose or direction at all – but not when you put them all together. Discover and look forward to seeing the bigger picture.

It may feel tempting to reach for the magic manifesting formulas again, but at the risk of repeating myself: this book is for all those who've tried positive thinking, affirmations and willpower and felt cheated. It presents a unique month-long programme of simple but practical and proven power moves – things you can start doing immediately – to change your life. It may be all you need to shift your life in the right direction, or you can use it as essential pre-manifesting prep. Either way, if you follow through on all the directives, it's eventually going to change all aspects of your life for the better. It just won't happen overnight. Temper your expectations from the start.

Not knowing yourself

Closely linked with unrealistic expectations is failing to know yourself well enough. For example, on a practical note, do you know what time of day is best for you to perform at your peak? Some of the power moves in this programme are specific to a certain time of day. So, if you don't think you're a morning person, then the morning power move suggestions may need a little personal adjustment to work for you or simply take a little longer for you to ace.

And do you know what setting is optimum for you to perform your power moves? Think about your living situation and what needs to be changed so that everything runs smoothly, or where you need to go to find peace and quiet if your power moves need to be performed in solitude.

Think about your personality too. Are you an introvert or an extrovert? Are you highly sensitive? Are you inclined to be practical and rational?

Get to know yourself a little better! Do some detective work. Personalize your power moves to fit your style and optimize your chances of success.

Too much like hard work

Laziness may rear its ugly head. When faced with the challenge of hard work to achieve our goals, many of us would rather seek the comfort of the familiar.

There's no time like the present to remind yourself that the familiar is not where the action and the potential for greatness lie. Smooth seas do not make skilful sailors. You must train yourself to get comfortable outside your usual comfort zone and to lose the fear of failure, setbacks or of putting yourself on the line. In different ways, all the power moves in this book will help you become fearless. Just stick with them. And when you don't feel like doing them, just count down from three to one in your head and make the choice to do them. Positive change really is as simple as that. It's your life. You and only you decide what you do with it. Apathy is a choice, but it won't make you happy so why choose it?

Too complicated

Another excuse can be that it's just too difficult. Well, you'll find that the 22 power moves in this book are super easy to learn and do, and can easily and effortlessly be slipped into your life, often without thought.

No time

Don't succumb to the tired, old "I haven't got time" excuse. As I've mentioned, the power moves in this programme aren't time-consuming, often taking just a few minutes. Even when you incorporate all 22 of them in your life, the investment of time will amount to no more than about ten minutes each day. And if you haven't got a few minutes to spare each day to work on your personal growth, you urgently need to rethink your daily routine and carve out that time for yourself, perhaps by getting up a few minutes earlier when everyone else is asleep!

Resistance to change

Resistance to change from yourself and others can also be a pitfall. Doing things differently may at first feel awkward – like writing with your non-dominant hand – but flex your determination and discipline muscles and remind yourself that Rome wasn't built in a day.

Practice and persistence make perfect. You've got this, and this book will constantly remind you of your own power and that the greatest learning happens when you're struggling and being challenged. Here you are, reading it, which proves you're keen to change your life. If you don't want to put in the effort to make that change, may I suggest you put this book down right now and go read another manifesting or "think your way to success" book? Perhaps that'll work out for you this time . . .

But it's not just your own resistance to change that may put on the brakes. You may well find that other people in your life struggle to adapt when they see you changing and becoming more action-focused. They may find it challenging to relate to you getting your life together, as misery loves company. You may even find that you lose friends or the support of others – but stand your ground. It takes true courage to live an impressive life. It's better to walk alone than to walk with those who won't let you stand tall and who prefer you to stare at the ground instead of gaze at the stars.

Lack of motivation

You can seriously counteract any lack of motivation by reminding yourself that you just need to keep going for four weeks. Those four weeks are going to pass by regardless, so you may as well make the best of them as they do so. Being told you need to do something forever can feel restrictive and daunting. But if you find yourself slumping, tell yourself that you'll check in again when the four weeks are up and if you don't feel any better you don't need to carry on. Keep things light and temporary as you begin this programme, and your ego won't put up such a fight.

The programme isn't going to feel challenging forever, because if you repeat your power moves every day for at least four weeks, something magical will happen. More and more of the power moves will start to feel automatic. You'll think about them less and simply do them. Rather like riding a bike or playing a musical instrument, at first it may feel insurmountable but with repeated and consistent practice, that feeling of ease and flow will take over. Elevating your day with power moves, and rising to the top as you do so, will become second nature.

Rising to the Top

All the suggested power moves will help you lead not just the successful life you deserve, but a potentially great life. A life you can be proud to live every single day, and which inspires others to double down and live their own great story too.

Resistance is futile. Let this energizing book take over your life, so that when you describe yourself and others describe you, it's as a person of their word – someone who does what they say they will, aka a great person of integrity. Let it motivate you to push the envelope and rise to the top, where you belong. Let it encourage you to give your small daily actions a chance to prove conclusively to yourself that you are what you repeatedly do. Let it be the highway from your comfort to your danger zone and all the exciting action, adventure and potential for greatness you'll find there.

What are you waiting for? Let's do this.

#DoSomething

I'm going to close this introduction in the same way I began, with another great and effortlessly simple-to-understand quote from an action-orientated movie, *Top Gun: Maverick*:

Don't think, just do.

Make #dosomething your mantra now as you raise the bar and take that first bold leap forward into your life-changing power move programme. And when that pesky self-doubt creeps in (and trust me, it will and that's okay, because you've got this), here's another iconic movie quote – this time from *Batman Begins* – with which to redefine and empower yourself in every possible way moving forward:

It's not who you are underneath,
it's what you do that defines you.[11]

THE FOUR-WEEK ACTION PLAN:
22 POWER MOVES

WEEK ONE: YOUR TIME TO WAKE UP!

This first week of power moves will help you set the new action-orientated tone for your daily life right from the get-go, the instant you open your eyes on waking. The eight power moves that follow should be performed within the first 30 minutes or so after waking and ideally before you begin your day in earnest. I'm going to call this time your "powerful me time", because it really is. Your actions in the first half an hour or thereabouts of your day set the tone and the direction for the rest of the day. What you do first thing matters a lot.

Can you remember the last time you woke up bursting with excitement about the day ahead, filled with energy and a sense of purpose, eager to jump out of bed? Maybe it was way back in your childhood on your birthday? Or perhaps the first day of a holiday or a new job? Or on your wedding day, or the morning of a special event?

This week aims to help you re-create that "it's a beautiful day" feeling on waking, when anything seems possible, so this isn't just a nostalgic memory or something that you experience sporadically, but your consistent everyday reality. It's just how you naturally tend to wake up.

You can jump right in and aim to do all eight power moves when you wake up tomorrow morning, but you might find that it's easier to adapt to them by easing them gradually into your morning routine and adding one or two power moves as Week One progresses. How you approach them is entirely up to you – just make sure that by the end of Week One you have all eight morning power moves in action.

Okay, enough said. Let's introduce you to your very first power move, which will begin the process of helping you wake up every single morning from now on eager to grab life and live the day ahead as it is meant to be lived – with passion, energy and purpose.

POWER MOVE NUMBER 1: Wake Up Naturally

What's your first action of the day?

Waking up, of course!

And how do you do it?

Alarm piercing your ears, heart-thumping, mind filled with dread, praying it isn't time to get up yet? Perhaps you hit the snooze button, begging your relentless alarm and its menacing tick-tock to gift you just a few more precious minutes' grace – like a child begging for a few more minutes before bedtime. Does this scenario sound all too familiar?

Why keep on diminishing yourself in this way every single morning when you really don't have to? Did you know it's entirely possible to train yourself to wake naturally instead and greet each day with a knowing smile rather than a grimace?

I'm fully aware that living alarm-free is a leap of faith and might not work for everyone. For example, if you're a shift worker, have early morning starts or are a busy parent, alarms may feel like your lifeline. The purpose of this power move is simply to make you aware of what your body is trying to tell you every morning when you wake up. To help you understand how beneficial it is for your well-being to work with your body rhythms, rather than against them – whether you continue to use an alarm clock or not.

Chances are your relationship with your alarm clock right now is toxic. Here's the good news. It's not you – it's your alarm! Alarms typically wake us during the most creative and liberating stage of sleep, REM, where all our wild and wonderful dreams incubate. Numerous studies have confirmed that waking abruptly during REM can result in low mood and anxiety during the day, not to mention that the shock of a ringing alarm clock can be as damaging to your heart, and therefore your physical well-being, as a mini stroke.[1,2] It's obvious when you think about it. In a matter of seconds, your body jolts from deep relaxation to wide awake, skipping the gentle liminal phases to help you transition naturally between sleeping and consciousness.

If you wake up in shock, your chances of having an empowered day dwindle dramatically. Remember the saying "getting out of bed on the wrong side"? Although it's not literally true – it doesn't matter which side of your bed you get out of – it's correct in some respects.

How you begin anything in life plays a key role in its future success. Think of it as being like putting the ignition key in your car: it's what lights everything you're going to do up and makes all future momentum possible. Of course, you can make your excuses – *I'm not a morning person, had a late night, a barking dog woke me up in the night, blah blah blah* – and while there may be some truth in this, the risk is when it becomes routine for you to start the day on the wrong side of the bed.

Your first action – waking up and how you do it – matters so much because it sets the tone for the whole day ahead. And this applies for both workdays and weekends. From now on, I want you to know that there are things you can do to change how you start your day. You can awake every morning feeling diminished and playing catch-up all day long. Or you can act right now and increase your chances of waking up feeling fully alive and ready to seize each new day.

Lights, Camera, ACTION

From personal experience and from coaching others, I know that this first power move – this simple shift in your routine – will make a huge difference. Typically, people are sceptical at first, but then when they give it a try, and train themselves over a period of several weeks to wake naturally without relying on an alarm, they experience a surge of creative and physical energy that they've never experienced before.

Not only do they know they've given their day the best possible start – because waking naturally is a sign of a good night's sleep and all the holistic healing and restorative benefits that offers – but they also feel empowered, because they've woken up on their own terms. They have shown themselves first thing that they are the master and commander of their own lives, and they're not at the mercy of external forces.

Whatever happens in the day ahead, you are where you belong – in the director's seat. You set the scene and the narrative for the day ahead. You make the choices that matter. You're the one who gets to say, "Lights, camera, ACTION!"

Wake badly and you can automatically handicap your chances of happiness and success. Wake positively and your chances of an empowering day skyrocket.

Acting Out: Case Study

Torri was the single mother of 18-month-old twins. She often felt her life was spiralling out of control. Her partner had vanished from the scene as soon as she fell pregnant, so she relied very much on her parents for support and moved back home to live with them to raise her family. She loved being a mother, but wanted to continue her teaching career and went back to work full time after her maternity leave. She relied on her parents and childminders while she was working. Despite thriving in her career and loving her life as a mother, Torri constantly felt fatigued and disempowered.

When I met her for the first time, I noticed dark circles under her eyes and asked her how she slept and woke up. She told me she was an anxious sleeper, because she worried every night that she might oversleep. She said on her first day back at work after maternity leave, she was so anxious she might not wake up in time, that she set up not just a phone alarm but a further three manual alarms on her bedside table. During the night she would often wake up to check that she had indeed switched on all those alarms.

Then in the morning she would wake up abruptly to the sound of all four alarms ringing simultaneously. She continued to repeat this night waking and traumatic waking-up pattern every single morning.

Hearing this, I wasn't at all surprised that her energy and motivation levels were low. I immediately encouraged her to change how she woke up each morning. As luck would have it, she was in the middle of her school summer holidays, so she had a good four weeks left to experiment with a new waking-up routine.

I suggested she ditch all her alarm clocks and visualize the worst-case scenario, which was that she did oversleep and arrived an hour or so late to work. I wanted her to know that it wouldn't be the end of the world if it did happen. Obviously, she wanted to make sure it didn't, so I encouraged her to put in place plans to wake naturally – and that is exactly what she did. And it worked. Within two weeks, she was waking up naturally at the time she wanted to and enjoying a quality night's sleep. Best of all, she told me how much it helped her to feel in control of her life again and on top of things at the start of the day, rather than overwhelmed by them.

However, the proof of the effectiveness of this power move wouldn't come until it was time for her to go back to work after the summer break. And I'm delighted to report that Torri never had to rely on a loud, ringing alarm clock again. On the rare occasion that she didn't wake up naturally, she used a gentle wrist alarm that was primed to go off if she wasn't awake in time, welcoming her into the day in a calmer way.

TAKE ACTION NOW

Your natural sleep cycle is controlled by your internal body clock – your circadian rhythm. This tells you when you feel tired and when you need to wake. If you're getting enough sleep, you will wake naturally and feel alert in the morning and have no trouble falling asleep in the evening. If you rely on alarms, this suggests that you're not getting enough sleep.

Skipping on time asleep to boost productivity will have the opposite effect. The more rested you are, the more productive you will be. Here's how you can increase your chances of both getting enough quality sleep and waking naturally each morning without needing an alarm.

- Your circadian rhythm is determined by your exposure to natural light. During the day make sure you let the light in for at least 30 minutes. Go outside for a walk, ideally in the morning, as getting your daylight fix then is optimum, but if that isn't possible open a window so light shines in. When it comes to bedtime, make sure it is dark enough, so your body knows it is time to fall asleep. (And keep an eye on the temperature too, as your body needs to cool down more than you think before sleep. The ideal temperature is around 15.6 to 20°C (60 to 68°F) for the most comfortable sleep.)
- Stick to a regular sleep schedule. Around eight hours sleep is considered optimum, but you need to find out how much sleep is right for you, as some people need a little more or less than that. Going to bed before midnight is recommended. If you feel tired, avoid lie-ins as they will give you jet lag without the holiday! Go to bed earlier instead.
- Have your last meal two hours before you go to bed. Your body needs time to digest food. If you're used to a snack just before sleeping, ensure it's easy to digest and light. The same is true for exercise: do it during the morning or afternoon, not before bedtime.
- Blue light from cellphones and screens has been shown to depress the release of melatonin, the sleep hormone, so try to avoid using screens an hour before bedtime.[3] Replace them with a good book or talking to loved ones or

friends instead. If you must use your phone, opt for some blue-light glasses that can protect your eyes from the light and boost your body's hormone secretion. And charge your phone as far away from your bed as possible at night.

- Try a wake-up light if you have to get up at a specific time in the morning. These lights can simulate a natural sunrise about 30 minutes or so before you need to get up, so you wake naturally.

- In addition to a wake-up light, you could try an alarm that has a natural sound, such as birds singing, rain falling or cows mooing at the exact time you need to wake up, as that's a gentler way to wake up. Or you could use an alarm that gently vibrates on your wrist.

- It goes without saying that stress is the enemy of everything, including a good night's sleep, so pay attention to your stress levels during the day and make sure your evening is as relaxed as possible.

- Before you go to bed, in that highly suggestible state between waking and sleep, tell yourself when you put your head on your pillow each night that you will wake up at a certain time. If you must get up at a certain time and need to set an alarm, tell yourself to wake up five or ten minutes before your alarm.

- Help yourself along during the day by intuitively guessing the correct time before you check your watch or phone to see the actual time. Notice how often you're correct. The more you do this, the more you'll be fascinated by the accuracy of your inner clock.

- Now that you know how crucial it is to wake up on the right side of bed, metaphorically speaking, take extra care to ensure your day begins in as calm and positive way as possible. And if you think you're not a morning person, learning how to wake naturally and to rely less on your alarm clock is how you can transform into one.

Above all, be patient with yourself. If you've relied on an alarm clock for decades, waking naturally won't happen overnight – and this power move may take up to a month or more to action – but if you keep working steadily (following the way of the tortoise) toward the end goal, you'll eventually get there. Be sure to keep a record of when and how you wake up each morning, so you can find out what works and what doesn't. And when you do wake naturally (and if you persevere, you will) please celebrate that.

You're one step closer to liberating yourself from servitude to your alarm clock. You're taking action to start your own engine and put yourself in the driver's seat of your life first thing.

Exciting!

POWER MOVE NUMBER 2: Scroll Your Dream Feed

Once you have woken up (naturally, I hope, from now on), what is the very next thing you typically do?

Perhaps you find you feel sleepy, but your head quickly fills with thoughts of the day ahead. You aren't quite ready to start the day, but do want to get ahead of your schedule and make sure you're on top of things. So, the perfect compromise is to reach out and grab your cellphone and check it while still lying in bed. It feels like a win–win: you're still relaxing and gradually waking up, but also "doing" something productive.

Be honest now, does the following scenario sound all too familiar?

Within moments of viewing your screen, you find that all those enticing notifications are impossible to ignore. After all, they could be urgent. You hastily review them all, read and answer emails, messages and texts and/or start scrolling your newsfeed to ensure you aren't missing out on the latest breaking news or gossip. Time flies and before you know it, you've been on your phone for twenty or more minutes. You jump out of bed, feeling behind before your day has properly begun.

Your intentions here may be good. After all, you want to check that you haven't missed any important messages from loved ones or colleagues, and you need to know what's happening in the world. But good intentions aside, the harsh truth is that reaching for your cellphone first thing is arguably the most disempowering thing you can ever do to yourself. Did you know that staying away from your phone for the first 30 minutes of your day is one of the simplest but also most crucial things you can do to dramatically change not just your day ahead, but your entire life for the better? Let's break this down.

Sleeping with your cellphone beside your bed and grabbing it first thing is an act of un-intentional self-sabotage. If you, like many people these days, carry your cellphone everywhere and can't bear to be parted, or feel lost without it and it's the very first thing you think about and want to interact with on waking, there is no easy way to say this: you're in a long-term co-dependent relationship with your phone. It may feel like your phone completes you, but whenever you become dependent on someone or something in this way, you diminish yourself. That's why this power move is going to ask you to dump your phone first thing and get intimate with a dream journal instead.

The purpose of this power move is once again to place you – yes, only you – centre stage in the morning. It's to help you understand that if you reach for your phone first thing, the message you are sending to the world, others and yourself (and you are always listening to the messages you send yourself) is that your needs are secondary. The needs of everyone and everything on your phone come first. When you wake up, your brain is in a twilight beta state for several minutes, sometimes longer, as you transition from sleep to waking alertness. What you do in this highly impressionable state will imprint on your brain and set the stage for the rest of the day.

While there can be no doubt cellphones are an incredible resource and a lifesaver in some instances, there's also no doubt that dependency on them is toxic. Many studies have linked cellphone addition to low self-esteem, anxiety and depression.[4] You may think you're not addicted to your phone, but if the first thing you do when you wake up is to check it, your phone – not you – is running your life. Even if you only look at it first thing and then during the day your use of it is light to moderate, by headlining your day with it, your cellphone will have placed itself centre stage in your mind, heart and life. The self-diminishing scene will have been set.

Every time you check the content of your phone, this triggers a stress response which releases cortisol into your body. And too much cortisol in your system is linked to anxiety and poor health. Is it a good thing to flood your system with that first thing? And it gets worse. Did you know that your brain also releases dopamine, a feel-good hormone, when you monitor your phone? But this dopamine hit is temporary, and your hungry brain always wants more of it, which means if you give your brain a dopamine fix first thing, it's going to crave more and more during the day. Your phone, not your intuition or your creativity, will be calling your name.

The more you limit your phone use, the less stress and anxiety you will experience from so-called "urgent" notifications.

Not checking your phone first thing in the morning will lay down a clear boundary with your device from the start, meaning you're far more likely to limit your use of it during the day and open yourself up to clear thinking, deeper creativity and meaningful connections with yourself and others. Not to mention, you'll be more present and in the moment, as you will be less distracted by futile comparisons with others on social media. And keeping your screen time under control, especially in the last hour before you go to bed sets yourself up for a good night's sleep too, which is essential for your holistic well-being.

Need any more convincing? The next time you travel on public transport, notice how many people are mesmerized, head down, staring zombie-like into their phones, barely noticing what is happening around them. Changing your life for the better includes taking back your power from your phone. Deliberately not reaching for your phone first thing and staying away from it for at least the first 30 mins of your day can be wildly liberating and personally empowering. Don't believe me? Try it when you wake up tomorrow morning and notice the impact it has on you.

If you've got into the habit of checking your phone immediately on waking, the best way to ditch this self-dismissing action is to replace it with a self-validating action. And that power move is writing in a dream journal on waking.[5]

Powered by Dreams

Moving forward, instead of reaching for your phone, please ensure you reach for your dream journal instead.

Your focus first thing must be on your own self-awareness and not the distractions and need for external validation that your phone will never fail to bring you. Your inner world is the place to find your strength, creativity, purpose and meaning. If you don't understand yourself from the inside out, you won't ever find that understanding from the outside in.

Dreams are the language your intuition and creativity speak, and there can be no better way to switch your focus from outside in to inside out than through writing down your dreams in a journal. Dreams are not random firings of the brain. Studies show they are a sign of holistic well-being and can help you with problem-solving, boost memory and creativity, and offer stress relief.[6] Best of all, consistently keeping a dream journal can help you understand yourself better, because your dreams really do shine the nightlight on your current mindset and whether it's helping or hindering you in your waking life. Understanding yourself is the beginning of all wisdom. And if you're one of those people who say they don't dream, let me reassure you that brain scans would show you do.[7] You're just not recalling your dreams and there are simple things you can do to improve your dream recall, as you'll soon discover.

Acting Out: Case Study

Mike was a busy digital content creator, working across many online platforms. Much in demand, he never seemed to be able to take a break from his work. His personal life suffered as a result. When I met him for the first time, he told me he was prone to bouts of insomnia. He was also feeling unfulfilled and restless, and the recent loss of his father had hit him badly, especially as his father had died a few months after Mike's own divorce. He knew that his busy work life had contributed to the breakdown of his marriage, but he also told me his work was the only thing that made him want to get up in the morning and start the day. If he didn't have his work, he said, he would just stay in bed.

I didn't even need to ask Mike if he checked his phone first thing in the morning; it was obvious that he did, as during our meeting he kept constantly checking his phone, even when it wasn't beeping. I asked him if he recalled his dreams on waking and he became very animated and spoke at length about his vivid dream life. Remarkably, as he was sharing his dreams, I noticed that even when his phone beeped, he ignored it and carried on sharing his night vision. This was the breakthrough I needed.

I suggested to Mike that he should write down his dreams first thing on waking, as they were incredibly creative. I told him about the impact of dreams on great movie directors, artists, musicians, inventors – and even scientists such as Einstein, who found inspiration for the theory of relativity from a vision in a dream. This really spoke to him, especially when I told him the plot of *Frankenstein* came from a vision Mary Shelley had in her dreams. I encouraged him to put a pen and paper beside his bed at night and avoid looking at his phone or any digital device for the first 30 minutes on waking, to give his own dreams and creativity a chance to surface.

A few weeks later, Mike told me that he was enjoying better quality sleep. Simply focusing on his dreams rather than his phone first thing had given him a sense of balance between his professional and personal life that had been completely lacking before. And when he woke up without dreams on his mind, he journaled his feelings instead. Indeed, he felt so passionate about his newfound focus on dream work on waking, he told me he was using his dreams as inspiration for the plot of his first novel, a paranormal thriller.

TAKE ACTION NOW

A full-blown cellphone detox simply isn't possible or advisable for most of us, as like it or loathe it, modern life revolves around the small black mirrors we hold in the palm of our hands. However, it's entirely possible to avoid checking your phone for at least the 30 minutes after waking, and this simple choice will put you and not your phone in charge of yourself and your waking life. Waiting in the wings to fill the void, by giving you something to do and focus on first thing, is your dream journal. If you're enslaved by your phone and new to dream journaling, you may need a few guidelines, so here's your dream action plan:

- Before you go to sleep, charge your phone away from your bedside table, so it's not within arm's reach on waking.
- Place a pen and piece of paper or a notebook with blank pages right by your bed. If it's going to be dark when you wake up, a flashlight or nightlight is advised. Make sure these are in within arm's reach on waking. (You can use a voice recorder but writing them down is preferable, as studies show it's a more immediate way to awaken your creativity.)[8]
- Rest your head on your pillow, and as you drift off to sleep, tell yourself you're going to recall your dreams on waking.
- On waking in the morning (or in the night), keep still for at least a minute or so with your eyes closed and recall your dreams, or the feelings and images associated with them.
- When symbols, images, stories, feelings surface in your mind, sit up, reach for your pen and paper and write them down. Don't try to make them make sense.

Simply thank your unconscious for its wisdom and for reminding you that you have an inner world. Let that wisdom settle and trust it will bring clarity when the time is right for you. Dream decoding is always better done with the benefit of hindsight, so avoid trying to force meanings first thing and return to your dream journal later in the day, or when you have the time to reflect.

- Let your dreaming mind know you've heard it. One way to do this is to use the power of action. Choose a harmless and gentle aspect of a dream, such as a colour or an object, and during the day, live out that aspect. For example, if there were flowers in your dream, you could buy yourself a bunch of flowers. If any more recollections arise later in the day, write them down too. See what associations and connections they trigger and if there's anything from your dream you can safely recreate in your waking life. Live your dream.

- If you wake and can't recall a dream, it's still important to reach for your dream journal. Write down the words "I feel", because how you feel on waking will have been inspired by the dreams you had, and this may trigger memories. Not recalling your dreams doesn't mean you don't dream, because brain scans show we all dream at least five or six times each night.[9] You've just gotten into the habit of forgetting them. If nothing still comes to mind, continue to document your waking thoughts and feelings.

- During the day, watch your stress levels and make sure you get plenty of the dream-recall vitamin B6 in your diet. B6 is found in sunflower seeds, tuna, turkey and dried fruit. Reading fiction, a spot of video gaming (as long as you game during the day and not just before bedtime, when it will be too stimulating) and giving yourself permission to daydream can all ignite clearer dream recall, too.

Above all, don't panic as everyone goes through periods when they don't recall their dreams. Simply trust that when the time is right you'll start to remember them again.

- Dreams speak the language of the unconscious, which is the symbolic language of the poet and the artist. To better understand them – and therefore yourself – you need to connect to your inner visionary and explore the deeper meaning beneath the surface of things. Dreams aren't linear, direct, literal or logical. For example, if you dream your teeth are falling out, you might consider in which area of your life you've been feeling "toothless" recently, or whether you're concerned about appearance or ageing.

- Remember too that your dreams dramatize your current mindset and what's helping or hindering your personal growth. Every aspect of the dream symbolizes an aspect of yourself and your perspective, as your dreams are created for you, by you and are all about you. If you don't like how your dreams make you feel on waking, they're an awesome reminder of the power of personal choice. You get to choose how you think, feel and react, and if you don't like how your choices make you feel, you always have the power within you to make changes now.

- Dreams can be an incredibly profound tool for greater self-awareness and there are plenty of books out there (I should know as I've written several) to help you learn how to use them as self-help tools and creativity hacks. Why not invest some time in learning more about them and by doing so, yourself? You won't regret it.

- Spending a few minutes writing down your dreams on waking and reflecting on their meaning, instead of being hypnotized by your phone, is one of the greatest gifts you can give yourself. Notice how liberated this activity makes you feel and how it ignites an awareness of your own worth and uniqueness, a sense of yourself as being mysterious and interesting. A perception of yourself independent of external validation. There truly is a treasure trove of inner creativity in the wonderland of your own dreams. Plunder and brainstorm them for a sense of deep meaning and direction. Keep reflecting on all the associations a dream symbol triggers within you until you feel an energy shift, because that eureka moment is likely to be the correct interpretation. A dream correctly interpreted will raise you up and never drag you down. And bear in mind that dreams are not for one night only. They are interpreted best as a series created for you, by you and all about you – as every symbol reflects an aspect of your mindset. So don't obsess about one dream in particular, but make sure you tune in night after night for the next gripping instalment in the great love story that is YOU.

Replacing phone checking first thing with writing in your dream journal is a game-changer. If you do this consistently for several days, you'll notice just how empowering it is. However, chances are you might also find that you don't want to go back to dependency on your phone for a sense of self-worth. Your phone becomes a useful tool but not a crutch, now that you've become fully aware of just how much of your identity and direction were previously delegated to it.

Why not take another step even further into your own personal power? Have a phone-free morning. Monitor your phone use during the day. Turn off unimportant notifications so you're less distracted and can focus on the present moment. At mealtimes, set aside your phone completely so you can listen to your body's hunger cues. Switch your phone to silent when meeting loved ones and friends and colleagues so you can be present for them.

If you aren't ready to do all this yet, that's fine. It's still early days. Give yourself a week or two to adjust to not reaching for your phone first thing. Once you get a handle on that, it'll become easier and easier for you to switch off during the day and also go to bed phone-free.

Let your last thing mirror your first thing. Switch off that cellphone at least 30 minutes before bed. You'll sleep better, because the content and light emitted from phone screens is overstimulating and can wake you up when you need to be winding down. Indeed, it's even better to end the day as you began it, by reaching for your dream journal. Before you go to sleep – when your brain once more enters that twilight and impressionable state – read about and brainstorm the meanings of the utterly unique creative content of your very own dream feed. So, when you drift off to sleep, dreams are on your mind, seriously increasing the likelihood they will also be on your mind on waking.

Ah, what dreams for you, dear visionary reader, may come!

POWER MOVE NUMBER 3: Rise Up and Skip

It's time to get out of bed, hopefully after you've woken up naturally and written down your morning dreams.

But how do you get up?

Let's say you roll over and lurch sideways. Then, when your feet eventually discover the floor and/or your slippers, you shuffle to the bathroom with your shoulders hunched, eyes half closed and head down, yawning quietly as you go. Your body language is small and low energy. The net result of this kind of repeated physical minimization first thing will come as no revelation. You are getting yourself out of bed on the wrong foot, on an insecure, physically diminished note.

Here's a necessary reminder that your actions don't always follow your feelings. The opposite is more often true than not, which is why standing tall and communicating energy on waking will help you feel more confident.

There is tremendous power in making yourself feel expansive the moment you get out of bed. If you tend to hunch when you get up, the message you send to your body and brain is that you're small and unimportant. Your body and mind are constantly listening to what your actions tell them to believe, so don't be shocked if the rest of your day reflects back to you that initial smallness or tone of unimportance you initially asserted.

Stretching and standing tall is a proven stress-buster and confidence-booster, and the first overt action you take in the day – typically, getting out of bed – may become the theme of your day.[10] You could very well be doing yourself a major disservice and experience decreasing confidence levels as the day develops if you act small on waking.

Harvard psychologist Amy Cuddy suggests that people who wake up by stretching their bodies in a "V" shape are more likely to feel confident than those who minimize themselves physically or stay as close as possible to the foetal position while getting up.[11] Treating yourself to an enormous stretch, perhaps with a battle-cry yawn, when you get out of bed puts you centre stage in your own life – the place you deserve to be. It helps you start the day on the right foot.

As well as the mood-boosting endorphin-releasing benefits, static or standing stretching will, of course, boost blood circulation to your entire body. After a good night's sleep, your muscles lose tone, and fluid tends to gravitate along your back. Stretching will help massage that fluid back into your limbs. Taking your muscles briefly outside their normal range also helps recalibrate them. There is everything to gain and nothing to lose by stretching big and standing tall when you get up.

Even more to gain when you add a skip (and/or a hum if skipping isn't possible) to your morning routine . . .

Skip a Happy Tune

The more skips you take the merrier – you can skip around your bedroom in a circle for a few moments if you like – but even if you can only manage a few skips that's enough. I'm not talking about rope skipping here. Absolutely not. I'm talking about skipping, just low-key skipping. Remember how much fun skipping was instead of walking when you were a child, how natural and happy it felt?

Although skipping is a great form of exercise, and highly recommended because it raises your heartrate but has less impact on your joints than running, the reason I'm asking you to add a few skips here and there to your morning routine isn't about burning calories; it's because skipping automatically connects you with your spontaneous, free-spirited, creative and childlike energy. It's also fun and impossible to skip without smiling. It's an instant mood-lifter. The perfect start to your action-packed day. Skipping is powerful medicine for body, mind and heart.[12]

Chances are you'll feel odd the first time you do this power move, but stick with it. Break out of your comfort zone and get over yourself. You won't ever regret it. Skipping not only connects you to your inner child, but it connects you to the beginner's mind at the start of your day and the willingness to learn new things. It's a way to experience all the benefits of play. Although life has many serious elements that should never be ignored, life is short and should also be filled with fun.

Should it not be possible for you to skip due to physical limitations, you can still reap the elevating benefits of this power move by making sure that when you get up in the morning, you look up rather than down at the floor. And instead of skipping, you could hum a happy tune to yourself. Humming is more impactful than simply listening to an energy-boosting song because the source energy is coming from within you. There's also plenty of evidence to suggest that humming can reduce stress, lower blood pressure and raise your mood.[13] Humming also leads to some unexpected psychological effects. These include increased body awareness and "decentring" – the ability to separate yourself from distracting thoughts and emotions and clear your mind.

That's why humming plays such an important role in meditation techniques that involve chanting, such as the Bhramari Pranayama technique, which involves humming while closing your ears with your fingers. One of the world's most chanted sounds – "omm" – involves a long hum at the end because it's believed to connect the chanter to feelings of inner peace.

Both skipping and humming are simple and natural to do. They feel great, boost mood and ease stress. So, when you get out of bed in the morning – or whenever you want to feel instantly better during the day – disarm yourself and silence your inner critic (and defy the expectations of others) by exercising your right to choose positive rebellion and breaking into a skip or a hum.

Acting Out: Case Study

Rachel was a respected health and well-being journalist who had recently gone freelance after 30 years working for leading media companies. It was a gamble for her professionally, but she wanted the freedom to choose her own features and interviews. She had a network of contacts in the industry and feature-writing offers and opportunities soon flooded in. Instead of feeling excited, she found herself suddenly unable to deliver assignments on time, although time management had never been a problem for her before. And when she did eventually deliver an assignment, she would be plagued with doubts and insecurities about it.

Self-sabotaging behaviour was stopping Rachel in her tracks, not just professionally but personally. She felt isolated from her former colleagues and unable to share her anxieties with her family and friends.

When I met her, I immediately noticed how small she made herself physically, how often she looked down and how intensely serious she was. I suggested she try stretching big first thing after waking and then skipping to her bathroom. Her initial reaction was shock. She told me that her fiancé would think she was crazy. I asked her to indulge me and let me know what his reaction was and how performing this simple power move impacted her mood and her day.

The following day, she told me that her fiancé had indeed burst out laughing, but in a good way. She also told me how much she'd loved to skip as a child and how good it felt to skip again. I asked her to listen to that feeling. It was the voice of her heart and every time she chose to listen to it – and ignored the logical part which worried far too much about appearances and what other people might think – she would grow stronger and more confident in herself and her own creativity.

In the weeks that followed, simply incorporating a big morning stretch and a bout of skipping into her morning routine became a game-changer for Rachel. It helped ignite the self-confidence and creativity she needed to thrive as a freelancer and, most importantly of all, to start every day with a smile. And her story gets even better, as a few months later Rachel got married. She proudly posted on her socials and tagged me in the enchanting scene of herself and her groom skipping hand in hand down the aisle!

TAKE ACTION NOW

Tomorrow when you wake up – and every morning from now on – don't just lurch out of bed and hunch and shuffle the way you've probably always done. Physically change everything about the way you get out of bed. Make yourself feel as big as possible on waking and then incorporate a skip and/or a hum into your morning routine.

- Stand up slowly, breathe in deeply and then reach as high as you can on your tiptoes, hands in the air toward the ceiling, and indulge in a mighty "V for victory" stretch. Take as much time as you need to stand in this expansive position.
- Notice how empowering it feels to stretch and become physically bigger than normal. To take up more space. This big morning moment is just for you. It's all about taking special care of yourself and reminding yourself how important and expansive you are.
- Then let your hands fall by your sides, take another deep breath and place them on your waist in a confident superhero pose, with legs apart. Feel big and confident. Make your presence felt. If you can't do your confidence pose in your bedroom, do it in your bathroom or

downstairs, but watch your posture. Push your feet slightly into the ground while straightening your spine and slightly elevating your head. Doing this stretches the body in two directions to maintain proper posture.

- During the day, if you need to decide on something and find yourself hunching your shoulders and minimizing your body, be sure to strike a pose and think and act big again. Even if you must fake it at the beginning, chances are it won't be fake for long. Your mind will always catch up with your body. And if you add a great big smile when you're doing this power pose, even if the smile is with your lips and not your heart, your brain won't know the difference. It will think you really are smiling. Give it a try.
- And if you need more inspiration check out the worldwide skipping organisation and the pioneering work of Kim 'Skipper' Corbin at www.iskip.com

Warning: Once you welcome skipping and/or humming back into your life, there may be no going back. It can become addictive, because you're physically reactivating your inner child and listening to the voice of your heart every time. You're exercising your own free spirit!

Stretching big as soon as you get up sounds deceptively simple but, it isn't as easy as you think, especially if you've got into the habit of minimizing yourself throughout the day by frowning and hunching your shoulders when checking phones or screens. Remember that your mind is led by your actions, so shrinking yourself first thing will almost certainly damage your self-esteem. Act fast to change that and tomorrow morning on waking, be sure to perform a big standing stretch and then treat yourself to a skip or a hum. If you can skip and hum at the same time all the better!

Starting your day with a big stretch and a skip and a hum will tell your mind that joy and positive energy are the hotly anticipated orders of the day. You'll probably notice that you can't do anything but smile as you skip and if you share your room with anyone, it will make them smile too. That's a win–win!

And why not seize the day and find other ways to incorporate a skip into your step. You can ask a child or a loved one to skip with you. You can skip around your living room. You can find ways to stealth skip when no one is looking! Depending on how self-conscious you feel, you might want to skip outside instead of talking a walk, or you could make a game of it and skip every time you see a green car or a bird. It's best to keep your skip low to the ground rather than bouncing too high in the air to conserve your energy if you're going on a long walk, but again do what feels natural and spontaneous to you. There are so many fun ways to incorporate skipping into your life again, now you know how empowering it is for your mind, body and heart.

In the great majority of cases, if you exercise your daring muscle and take your newfound love of skipping outside, you'll be amazed how liberating it feels. Chances are you may feel nervous about doing it at first, because adults for some inexplicable reason are allowed to walk, run and fall but not to skip. Being outdoors isn't mandatory, as stretching and skipping indoors will energize and empower you, but if you're able to take a skip outside your comfort zone in the fresh air, you won't regret it. Magic happens outside your comfort zone and that is exactly where you'll find yourself if you take a leap of faith and dare to skip and/or hum with conviction outside.

Often, you'll find that other people will ignore what you're doing because it confuses them. If you're lucky, you may find one or two people who give you a thumbs-up and a big smile. You're reminding them that it's never too late to connect to our inner child and have a happy childhood. Should passersby raise an eyebrow, frown or be rude, that's on them – not you. If they aren't feeling good about themselves, seeing someone else act in a carefree and joyful manner may trigger them. But there's no law against skipping and/or humming. You are showing yourself and others that being an adult can be fun.

If you're constantly concerned about what other people think, this might be one of the most empowering power moves for you. Walking your talk is all about freeing yourself from the expectations and judgements of others and being authentically yourself. If you can confidently skip down a pathway while humming a happy tune to yourself, without a care for what others think, the only way ahead now for you is onward and upward. It's your time to rise up – and skip!

POWER MOVE NUMBER 4: Make Lemonade

Okay, you've got out of bed, ideally on the right foot. What happens next?

Your usual "get ready for the day" routine, of course, whether that be a shower and getting dressed followed by breakfast (or no breakfast if you're pushed for time) and perhaps a spot of exercise if you're able to squeeze that in too.

You've likely repeated the same routine so many times it passes in a blur. You may even struggle to know how it makes you feel or even remember doing it. This is because you're on autopilot and you mind likely hasn't fully woken up yet, so your focus is on being as efficient as possible and just getting it all done in time. Given what you now know, and how crucial the actions you take in the first 30 minutes or so after waking are for setting the empowered tone for the rest of your day, this mindless start to your morning clearly isn't serving your best interests.

Happily, there's a simple way to ensure your morning routine is done with clear-eyed intention and vibrant focus instead. Just stand or sit still and drink a full glass of warmish water, ideally with a slice of lemon or a hint of freshly squeezed lemon juice, before you launch into your usual morning routine.

Your body consists of up to 70 per cent water. Drinking enough water is therefore essential for optimum brain function and for ensuring all your cells, tissues, muscles and organs get the nutrients they need to keep your body going strong. It's impossible to understate the importance of adequate hydration for your holistic well-being, especially first thing in your day, when you've been on a mini fluid fast while asleep.[14] The last time you drank water may have been up to eight or nine hours ago, or more. That's a long time for your body and brain to be deprived of it.

If you want to think, feel and look your best (water flushes out those toxins, which means your skin will benefit, too), the message of this power move could not be clearer: drink a full glass of water or two as soon as you get up, before you start getting ready for the day ahead. And, if you add a slice of lemon or a hint of freshly squeezed lemon juice to your morning glass of water, your body and mind will get all the phenomenal digestive, immune, energy and health-boosting benefits of lemon power to turbo charge you first thing, too.

Drink in the Benefits

Drinking enough water is something we can easily neglect to do. Time to remember now what you learned in biology class at school . . . You can't live without water, as every organ in your body craves it, with your brain being the thirstiest. Your body needs adequate hydration to carry out many essential functions and processes, such as regulating its internal temperature and keeping cells alive. Your brain needs it all the time, because your brain is up to 85 per cent water. Water gives your brain energy to function, including your thought and memory processes. Water is also needed to produce hormones and neurotransmitters in the brain. You can't think clearly or concentrate properly if you're dehydrated.

Water is, of course, the basis of all our bodily fluids, such as saliva, blood, sweat, tears, joint fluid and urine. To reinforce the fact that water is the elixir of life, here (listed by medicalnewstoday.com) are just some of our physical processes that can't function without getting enough of it every day:

- aiding in digestion by forming saliva and breaking down food
- moistening mucous membranes

- helping to balance the pH of the body
- lubricating joints and the spinal cord
- helping the brain make and use certain hormones
- helping transport toxins out of cells
- eliminating waste through urine and breath
- delivering oxygen throughout the body.

On the other hand, dehydration can also cause severe medical problems – from poor concentration and low blood pressure, to liver and kidney failure. We can live without food for up to three weeks but the longest we can survive without water is just a few days. Dehydration happens without you even realising it can happen. You can swiftly move from feeling tried and thirsty on the first day without water, to organ failure by the third.

Without water, the body cannot eliminate waste effectivity through urine, sweat and breath, and toxins will build up, harming the kidneys, which process the removal of toxins from the body. If the kidneys fail, the toxins build up even further, ultimately causing widespread organ failure and death if left unchecked.

All these dehydration disaster scenarios aren't to alarm you. I've shared them simply to help you to remember the healing power of water. If you feel sluggish and lack energy, are prone to headaches and find it hard to concentrate, or if you suffer from periods of fuzzy thinking, stiff joints or hot and cold sweats, there could be many reasons and you're always strongly advised to check what could be causing these symptoms with your doctor. But one simple cause or contributing factor you can easily diagnose and eliminate for yourself is dehydration.

You probably know how crucial drinking enough water is for your well-being, yet one obstacle could be the tedium of it, or perhaps you simply don't enjoy the taste. Adding a slice of lemon can significantly improve the taste and make drinking water more enjoyable; even more importantly, lemon juice is incredibly beneficial for our holistic well-being. I should know as I once wrote a book dedicated to the nutritional power of lemons called *The Lemon Juice Diet*, with a foreword by Dr Marilyn Glenville.[15]

To cut a long story short, there are a lot of proven health benefits to drinking lemon water every day, which can help with anything from your skin to your mood to regulating your weight.[16] There's a reason why if you have ever been to a health farm or fasting retreat, the first drink of your day is typically lemonade. This is due to the immune-boosting, high vitamin C, antioxidant and citric acid content that can aid digestion, prevent kidney stones, help freshen breath, give you better skin and boost mood, energy and immunity.

So, case closed: not only will adding a slice of fresh lemon improve the taste of water, meaning you're more likely to drink it up each morning, but lemon water is also really, really good for you, bringing a whole new meaning to that self-help cliché "if life gives you lemons, make lemonade"!

Acting Out: Case Study

Single mum Dina was a much-in-demand yoga coach. As she was a ball of energy, this was a natural career choice for her. In addition to her yoga teaching schedule, she created a lot of content for her clients on her website and popular social media channels. When she wasn't teaching, she spent many long hours on her computer. A self-confessed perfectionist, she was her own worst critic and constantly revised her online content to ensure it was the best it could be.

She told me that she was suffering from morning headaches and acute stomach pain. She was applying all her yoga knowledge to try to ease it and limit her computer time and although these common-sense steps certainly helped in the short term, the unexplained pains always seemed to come back. She had visited her doctor, who gave her a physical examination but could find nothing wrong. They suspected the problem might be hormonal and connected with her monthly cycles. She was advised to keep a diary for four weeks to see if any patterns emerged and if that didn't help, she would need to see a specialist.

I asked Dina to describe the stomach pain, and she said that when it hit it was worse than childbirth. Immediately, I felt I might know the cause, because the previous year I had used the same "childbirth" description when I'd experienced serious stomach pains and been admitted to hospital. The pains had been sporadic at first, happening every few days. Typically, they would pass in an hour or so, and I would carry on with my day, thinking it was just one of those things and I needed to destress. Then, one afternoon, the pain became so crippling, I couldn't even stand. When I checked into the emergency room at my local hospital, and they tried to give me pain killers I could not even get them down my throat. I vomited everywhere.

I was admitted to hospital for observation and put on a drip for 24 hours. Within a few hours, the pain eased and it had gradually subsided completely by the end of the day. When the consultant studied my scans, he told me that I'd recently passed a large kidney stone and that was why I'd been in such pain. The consultant explained that kidney stones are caused by a build-up of materials and salts that form inside the kidneys. Typically, they dissolve and pass out of the kidneys via urine, but if you're severely dehydrated, as I was at the time, then it meant a world of excruciating pain. In short, the cause of my stomach pains – and the mind-numbing morning headaches I was also experiencing at the time – wasn't stress but chronic dehydration. I had forgotten the power of water.

Ever since that wake-up call, I started to religiously drink a glass of water on waking and to ensure I kept up my water intake during the day.

I asked Dina now how much water she drank. She told me she didn't drink much tap water as she didn't like the taste, but she did drink lots of juices and herbal teas. I urged her to carry on talking to her doctor, and also to make sure she drank a glass of water or two in the morning on waking and to drink water during the day every time she had her juices and teas. To make the water more palatable, I told her to add a slice of lemon.

Four days later, Dina got in touch to tell me that it felt like a miracle cure. Her symptoms had improved dramatically, and she was waking up clear-headed for the first time in months. She couldn't believe that, with her knowledge of holistic well-being, she had missed the blindingly obvious and that the answer lay in something as simple as drinking enough water.

TAKE ACTION NOW

There are notable symptoms of dehydration to be alert to, such as a dry mouth, feeling thirsty, morning headaches and unexplained stomach pains, but when you notice these symptoms, dehydration has already set in. Dehydration can happen very quickly and creep up on you unawares. By far the best way to prevent the damaging impact of dehydration on your brain and body is prevention. Don't wait until symptoms set in. Make sure from the moment you get up in the morning that you're aware your brain and body crave water, and that for the rest of the day you remain on top of your water intake.

- If you often feel mentally sluggish in the morning, a glass or two of water with a slice of lemon or a few drops of freshly squeezed lemon juice can often remedy that. Chances are that your first drink in the morning is a juice or a tea or coffee, but from now on make sure that first drink is water with a hint of lemon. Nothing beats a simple glass of lemon water for flushing toxins from the system and giving us renewed mental energy and focus. It will help you start your day in a sparkling and clear-eyed manner. Ensure you drink your lemon water before you get dressed or have breakfast and as you drink it, consciously notice how refreshing and energizing it is. Remind yourself how essential water is for your health and how lemons can add zest to the start of the day. This knowledge will improve the taste.

- Your morning glass of lemon water should ideally be warm. Resist the tendency to add ice or drink chilled water. Your body has just woken up and ice will be too much of a shock to your system and limit the amount you're able to drink. Room temperature water is fine. It should ideally come from a glass, tap or water-filtered source that is clear of pollutants; avoid water in plastic containers, as they leach harmful chemicals into the water inside them and aren't environmentally friendly.

- If you're not used to drinking a full glass of water first thing, count down from three to one mentally and then on the count of one just drink it up.

- Although other liquids such as herbal teas, juice and broth can aid hydration, as can water-based foods such as fruits, berries and vegetables, none of these fluid sources are as efficient in hydrating your brain and body as water with a hint of lemon.

- Experts recommend drinking about three litres of water a day, which is around eight full glasses of water. That sounds like a lot, but it can easily be done if you drink a glass of water or two when you wake up, and then make sure you monitor your water intake during the day to ensure you're adequately hydrated. Drinking a glass or two of water before meals and snacks is one way to do this. You can also measure out your day's water intake in a non-plastic jar or glass bottle to make sure you drink the right amount. If you take that route, make sure you carry a few slices of lemon with you, too, in an air tight container.

- Be aware that several factors may impact how much water you need, and these include your age, activity levels (how much you sweat), your height and weight, the climate you live in and how many water-based foods (such as fruit, vegetables, soups and juices) are in your diet. If your diet is rich in dry, salty, spicy or packaged foods, this can worsen dehydration, as can alcohol and caffeine consumption, which both cause excessive urination. If you're a regular tea and/or coffee drinker, make sure you drink even more water.

- It's rare but possible to become too enthusiastic with your water drinking and consume too much. To make sure you're drinking the right amount, the best way is to check your urine regularly. If it's dark yellow or amber, you're dehydrated and need to drink more water. If it is light or pale straw yellow, and a rather similar colour to your morning lemon water drink, you're doing fine on the water front. Any other shade, be sure to see your doctor immediately.

Don't forget that drinking enough water is essential for tear formation. Although we cry when we are sad or in pain, tears can be healing. Crying is cathartic and we also cry when we feel happy or need to let go of what no longer serves us. There will be more on the healing benefits of tears in Power Move Number 10, but for now – what are you waiting for? Raise a glass of water, add a hint of delicious freshly squeezed lemon juice or a slice of fresh lemon – and drink that liquid gold up!

POWER MOVE NUMBER 5: Chill Yourself

Time now to start getting ready for your action-packed day ahead! I'm going to assume you've hydrated yourself with plenty of water and perhaps had a healthy breakfast if you prefer to eat while still in your sleepwear. You may even have treated yourself to some morning exercise. Whatever the order of your morning routine, you'll inevitably find yourself in your bathroom at some point, brushing your teeth and hair and having a shower or a wash before you get dressed. If you've actioned the previous four morning power moves, you'll be feeling far more awake than usual, but there is something you can do now that will be a breakthrough when it comes to feeling utterly reinvigorated at the start of your day.

First, though, let's have a think about your usual routine . . . You probably turn on your shower or your tap and wait until the water is invitingly warm. Then you step inside or wash yourself, relishing the cosy feeling that warm water brings to your skin and body. The sensory stimulation triggered by the water temperature on your skin is so soothing. If you shower, you may find yourself spending a few more minutes in there than you really need to, because it's so relaxing. The warm water helps relieve any muscle tension and the sound and feel of the water creates a calming effect, reducing anxiety and promoting a sense of well-being. You even may favour a hot shower, as you find that warm showers don't elevate your body temperature or mood enough. Either way, you know what temperature feels best for you and you are re-energized afterwards, having cleansed yourself of both physical dirt and mental stress. It's your blissful but temporary sanctuary time.

But what if I told you that the warm or hot water temperature you routinely crave on waking isn't doing you any favours in the long term? Warm or hot showers can calm your nervous system, ease stress, lower blood sugar and induce the release of relaxation hormones. They can also boost creativity and be a mini mediation, but you've got the timing wrong. The ideal time to reap the rewards of a warm or hot shower is before you go to bed, to prepare you for a great night's sleep; not first thing in the morning when you need to daydream and chill out a little less and get going a little more.

The ideal temperature for your morning washing routine is on the cold side of the tap or faucet.[17]

Cold Therapy

If the hot water runs out and suddenly turns cold when you're taking a shower, maybe the shock will make you'll curse or scream, but it could be doing you a world of good. You will be unintentionally experiencing cold therapy or cryotherapy. Like many beneficial things, it may be tough and a bit grim, but it's seriously good for you.

Cold therapy aims to cool down your body tissues for therapeutic reasons. It can ease any inflammation and muscle soreness. You're likely to be already familiar with ice-pack treatment for injuries and muscle pain. The logic behind this is that the ice encourages your blood vessels to constrict and when this happens, blood flows to your body's vital organs and becomes oxygen- and nutrient-richer in the process. When your body heats up again, blood vessels expand and the oxygenated blood moves back to tissues, flushing out the inflammation that causes muscle soreness. Ice packs can also dull nerve transmission to your brain and thereby ease pain.

Cold therapy also boosts immunity. The shock of cold water can stimulate blood cells that fight infection and protect us from viruses. Indeed, one study from the Netherlands showed that people who switched to cold showers for a minimum of 30 seconds for three months took almost 30 per cent fewer sick days from work than people who didn't switch to cold showers.[18] There is also preliminary research that shows cold therapy can elevate mood, counter grief and depression and even protect from dementia.[19]

Cold water puts the body under strain – it goes into survival mode, working hard to maintain its core temperature. This stimulates our body to increase blood flow circulation. Whenever circulation increases, freshly oxygenated blood is redistributed around your body. Over time, blood circulation becomes swifter, which is good news for keeping our blood pressure levels healthy. There may even be a slight calorie-burning metabolism boost when you take a cold shower, because your body expends energy trying to stay warm in it.

Although there are proven health benefits, at the start of your day the standout benefit is greater alertness. Taking a cold shower will most definitely wake you up mentally and physically. It resets your brain and reinvigorates your body. Best of all, it will increase your emotional resilience during the day ahead.

You've also deliberately chosen to get outside your physical comfort zone and take the road less travelled, as by far the easiest and most comfortable path to take is to step into that inviting hot shower. Progress is only made outside your comfort zone. Each time you practise a little cold water therapy, you're training both your body and your mind to get more comfortable managing chaos, facing fears and taking risks.

Acting Out: Case Study

Liam was always taking sick days off work from his job as an engineering manager. This was causing problems with his management team, as a lot of his duties included planning, designing and supervising teams that would benefit most from in-person rather than online consultation with him. On top of that, he suffered from panic attacks whenever faced with pressure at work and this, compounded with his many requests for sick leave, was undermining his ability to convince his employers that he should keep his position.

When I met him, I noticed how many layers of clothing he was wearing and asked him if he wanted to hang up his jacket, but he refused, saying he couldn't stand the cold. It was early September and by no means chilly inside or out. Intuitively, I sensed that his strong feelings about being cold were like a mirror reflecting all his fear and uncertainty back to him. Without hesitation, I urged him to take a cold shower every morning for the next 30 days. It wasn't easy to convince him, as he told me that he was prone to being ill and surely cold exposure would make that worse. I told him to be sensible and not take a cold shower when he was unwell or experiencing symptoms, but to give it a try on those days when he was healthy. I shared the research on the benefits of cold water therapy, and this encouraged him to take a leap of faith into the cold.

Not only did Liam give it a try, he fell hopelessly in love with the theory of taking cold showers and embraced it in a way that surpassed my expectations. Besides boosting his alertness first thing, it gave him a sense of accomplishment and resilience he didn't know he had. Best of all, he hasn't had a sick day off work since.

TAKE ACTION NOW

The following suggestion may feel a little too radical at first, as chances are you prefer your shower to be as hot as possible in the morning. Indeed, the idea of a cold shower might fill you with dread, but if you give it a chance it really is worth it for the invigorating high you'll get afterwards. So, if you are keen to take a leap of cold faith, here's what to do . . .

- When you switch on your shower in the morning aim to keep your water temperature on a colder or lower setting than you usually do. Take things slowly. Every cell in your body will be craving the familiar warmth. The first time you do this, you might want to start with just 10 seconds of cold water and build up from there the following day with 20 seconds. Keep increasing the amount by 10 seconds as each day passes until you hit one minute. After that, you can extend it to two or three minutes. If you simply can't bear the thought of stepping into a cold shower or taking a full-blown cold shower in the morning, start your shower with warm water and then go cold for the final 30 seconds or so of rinsing.
- You will, of course, feel a bit of a shock when the cold water first hits your skin. This increases your oxygen intake, heart rate and circulation and therefore your alertness. You may also notice after a few days of morning cold showers that your skin glows and your hair feel healthier, because unlike hot water, cold water doesn't dry out the sebum layer, a naturally lubricated barrier that provides protection for your skin and hair.
- Expect to have your breath taken away, quite literally, when you first step into a cold shower. Your breathing will be uneven and frantic. Inhalations will be short and there may be virtually no exhalation, but you want to focus on those exhalations until you can get them under control. And when you do get them under control, this is when a feeling of deep calm will rush over you. When we can find a sense of control and calm in the chaos that cold water induces within us, it can be found anywhere.
- If you don't own a shower or prefer not to shower first thing, that's okay. You can still get some of the benefits of cold therapy simply by splashing your face for 10 or 20 seconds with cold water from the tap in your bathroom sink.

- Of course, hot showers and baths have benefits too, but those benefits are more suited to the evening, when relaxation rather than alertness is the order of the day. If you work out daily and like to shower after that as well, you might want to alternate between a hot and cold shower to reap the benefits of both. Go for three minutes hot and one minute cold and repeat the pattern a few times, making sure you always end with cold.

Warning: Cold therapy is entirely safe if you're healthy, but if you have any health conditions or concerns, or are elderly, please make sure you contact your doctor before experimenting with it. It may not be the best option if you feel cold when you wake up either, as it will make you feel even colder and increase the amount of time it takes for your body to warm up. It's also not advised if you're sick or have a cold or flu, as the cold temperature might put too much strain on your immune system, which then needs to divert its energy from fighting viruses.

If you find that cold therapy energizes you, then you can go all in with a cold bath and submerge everything but your head and neck in cold water. And if you're brave enough, there are always ice baths, which some athletes, motivational coaches and celebrities swear by because of how they boost focus and energy levels. However, that's pretty extreme and unnecessary. You can get a lot of benefit from simply making sure your last shower rinse is a cold one, or by splashing your face with cold water. And being mindful that feeling cold can be good for you, perhaps turn down your central heating a notch if it is medically safe for you to do so, to help keep your alertness levels high and your energy bills lower.

Be aware that although you'll feel on high alert, it may take a while before you can say you "enjoy" a cold shower in the moment. The "enjoyment" and sense of accomplishment only kick in when you switch off that cold shower and start to dry yourself afterwards. This is all good. You've demonstrated to yourself in the first few minutes of your day that you have discipline and determination and can focus on long- rather than short-term reward.

It can feel like chaos to step outside your comfort zone, but it's the only place to learn about yourself. It may feel like a battle every time you turn the hot tap down, but when it's over you will feel victorious. You'll realize that you can find balance and calm despite facing external pressures. If you can breathe deep calm into the cold, you can do it in any difficult situations that arise at work or home. Your daily battle and victory in a cold shower and focusing on controlling your exhalation will help you feel more in control and calm under pressure in your day ahead. You can master your fear of the cold and any other chaos life throws at you.

POWER MOVE NUMBER 6: Worth Your Wear

Morning has well and truly broken for you now, especially if you have successfully actioned the previous five power moves. Let's press on and choose your outfit for the day and get dressed.

We all know we shouldn't judge a book by its cover or a person by the clothes they wear, but the reality is that lots of us unconsciously still do this. Be honest now: when choosing to read a book, how influential is the cover art in swaying your decision, especially if you're in hurry? Think about this. If you're out and about and find yourself lost, but your phone isn't giving you the right directions so you need to ask a stranger walking by for directions, to what extent does the way they dress influence your decision to approach them in the first place?

Of course, you can only know the true measure of a person's integrity and character by getting to know them on a deeper level over a period of time. First impressions can be so very wrong but they really do count. (Read or re-read Jane Austen's *Pride and Prejudice* to better understand that universally known truth.) And those first impressions don't just count when it comes to other people and how confident you feel around them, they count when it comes to how confident you feel about yourself every single time you look in the mirror.[20]

Perhaps you've gotten into the routine of wearing virtually the same items of clothing each day, so you don't have to think too much in the morning. After all, it worked for Steve Jobs, and Mark Zuckerberg famously said that wearing the same outfit each day was one less decision he needed to make in his crazy, busy life. Or perhaps you have a weekly rotation system? Or perhaps you simply grab whatever you can find or what you feel will match the occasion or help you blend in? Or perhaps comfort is more important to you than quality, or vice versa? And when it comes to cosmetics, if you wear them are you minimalist in your approach, or is it impossible for you to leave the house without full make-up?

None of the fashion scenarios described here are right or wrong, or better or worse, as what works for one person when it comes to clothing and make-up choices won't necessarily work for another. This power move isn't about decision fatigue or dressing for success or encouraging you to change your appearance in any way. It's simply about dressing with confidence, dignity and a dash of personal flair. It is choosing to wear what makes you feel authentic and powerful. In other words, you're wearing clothes that empower you; your clothes aren't wearing you.

Dressing Up

Like it or loathe it, your clothes reflect who you are and what you want to be. People who are confident will ensure their clothes send that message of self-respect to others.

Clothes can also impact your performance. Wearing comfy pants and a T-shirt will likely put you in a sleepy mode or get you primed for exercise, depending on what you associate these items with. Best of all, your clothing choices also give you a fun outlet to express your personality.

Remember when you were a child and played dressing-up – what fun it was to role play and experiment? To change the first impressions people had of you? Power Move Number 6 hopes to reconnect you to that playful spirit when it comes to your clothing choices each morning. Rather than looking at your wardrobe and fitting your personality around the choices there or relying on labels, logos and brands to define how confident you feel about your appearance, instead you think first about what image you want to present and then make clothing choices to reflect that.

This doesn't necessarily mean changing your wardrobe entirely – it can be as simple as ensuring the colour choices match whatever vibe you want to project that day. And making sure that some aspect of your appearance is an upgrade and slightly better than the occasion requires. When you dress in a way that makes you appear that you're on top of your game, chances are you won't be left behind.

There is no doubt that what we wear matters, not just because first impressions count but also because it impacts our confidence levels. Research backs this up and shows that dressing for success works, and impacts how other people evaluate us.[21] (If you've ever gone to an event in your casual clothes and everybody else was dressed up, or vice versa, you'll likely have felt personally diminished and know the reality of this.)

Obviously, at some point in your life, you want to have enough confidence to not let what you wear dent your confidence in any way – and this power move hopes to play its part in getting you there – but let's face it, absolute self-belief is a work in progress even for the most confident dresser. Clothes, accessories and hair and make-up decisions can all give us an instant boost when our self-belief needs a helping hand. Even if you're fully aware that your self-belief shouldn't be dependent on these externals, there's nothing wrong with letting your clothes carry you forward.

One way to ensure your clothes quite literally help you walk your talk is to make sure that they are always well fitting, clean and ironed if need be. As a rule of thumb, dress slightly better than you need to for the occasion, as this will impress on yourself and others that time spent with you is always significant. If you can, watch a few episodes of the TV series Downtown Abbey and note that glorious tradition of getting dressed for dinner each evening. The characters aren't going out anywhere and often don't have guests, but as a mark of respect for themselves and their family they dress to the nines.

Don't confuse getting dressed to the nines with wearing designer clothes and expensive jewellery, though. It is simply about making the very best of what you can afford and adding a hint of originality. It's about making sure something in your wardrobe is unique and meaningful to you. It is imprinting your personality on your clothes, rather than your clothes defining you.

Acting Out: Case Study

Mindy suffered greatly with body image issues as a child, but found respite when she became a goth and started routinely wearing black. Not only did black make her feel slimmer and taller, but she also felt it gave her an identity and expressed her personality. I met her when she was in her mid-twenties, and she wanted to understand the meaning of recurring dreams she was having. In those dreams, she told me the colours were so vibrant, but despite this she woke up in the morning feeling apathetic and despondent. She wanted to know how her dreams could help her create an inner shift.

I congratulated her on looking to her dreams for a sense of inner power and encouraged her to continue. However, I said that she might also benefit from an instant mood boost and approach things from the outside in, so there was a two-pronged attack. I asked how she felt about matching the colour vibrancy in her dreams with the colours she was drawn to in her waking life.

Black had been Mindy's go-to wardrobe choice for over six years, and I knew that she couldn't immediately shift to wearing all the colours of the rainbow, so I asked her to add a colourful jewellery item to her daily wardrobe. She wanted to know why I was suggesting this instead of helping her understand her dreams, and I explained that her colourful dreams needed an outlet and to be lived in waking life.

I also showed her some of the research behind the psychological impact of colour. I reassured her that there was nothing negative about wearing black – like any colour, it has both negative and positive potential – but wearing just the one colour all the time was seriously limiting her creative potential and what and who she was attracting into her life. In the case of black, it's the colour of mystery and the unconscious, but it can also point toward blockage and keeping things hidden that need to be expressed. Not to mention that black can appear intimidating. This immediately made sense to her.

In coming months, black remained a staple of Mindy's wardrobe, but she started to enjoy adding a flair of colour through her choice of bags, jewellery and make-up. Indeed, she became something of a colour expert and told me how every morning she would tune in to the energy and associations of a certain colour she was going to add to her wardrobe to ensure it was the right vibe for her day ahead. Getting up in the morning and enjoying getting dressed felt meaningful and empowering to her again. She was wearing her worth.

TAKE ACTION NOW

Dressing well is an art worth learning because it'll make you feel your best and at the same time gain the attention and respect of others around you.

- Tomorrow morning when you get dressed, or if you are super-organized and like to lay your clothes out the night before, ensure that you choose items that don't just match the activities you have planned for that day, but that they are slighter better than the occasion demands. For example, if you're spending a day at the office, you could wear a pair of shoes or a coat that you usually reserve for formal occasions. If you're meeting friends, wear that dress or outfit that you've been saving for special occasions. You are communicating without saying a word that you feel both yourself and others are worth making an effort for and signalling to them that time spent with you is a big deal. Trust me here: you'll never regret being the best-dressed person in the room.

- Make sure your hair is always clean and as groomed as possible. If you want to wear make-up, ensure it's skilfully applied. If you are spending a day at home don't let your desire for comfort override your sense of style, as you're still going to meet yourself in the mirror. As mentioned earlier, clothes have the proven ability to impact how you perform and to boost your confidence. Paying attention to what you wear each day will help you believe in yourself. It won't solve all your problems, but it'll at least make you feel that conquering them is possible.

- Remember that this isn't about wearing expensive clothes or layers of make-up and hair styling. If your self-worth is entirely dependent on this sort of superficial stuff, you need to revisit power moves 1 to 5 repeatedly until you feel you're worth your wear and not the other way around. It's about showing and dressing up for both yourself and others. It's about getting that balance between knowing your appearance matters yet not being defined by it. It's about respecting the occasion with your clothing choices, but also making sure you always bring along your individuality.

- Choosing items of jewellery or accessories that are uniquely you is one way to express and encourage belief in yourself, and you likely do that already, but I hope this power move will remind you of their Dumbo's feather value. In the beloved Disney movie of the same name, Dumbo is a baby elephant with huge ears who's told by some friendly crows that if he carries a feather in his trunk, he can fly with them. It takes a crisis for him to learn that the feather wasn't magically making him fly, he could fly all the time. He just didn't believe he could. If you're aware the power is in you, there's no harm done at all. We all need a boost sometimes. On days when I feel in need of a little lift, I always wear my three inexpensive crystal bracelets – one made of rose quartz as a symbol of self-love, one made of carnelian for self-belief and the third is amethyst for intuition. Somehow, wearing them reminds me of the importance of self-love, self-belief and intuition in my life and it just helps. I can't explain why but it does. Not all irrational beliefs are an evil. But perhaps the simplest way to help you feel good in what you wear is to pay extra-special attention each day to your colour choices.

- The colours you choose to wear send both you and all those you encounter subliminal psychological messages. Learn all about the psychological power of colour and then make the colours of your clothes speak for you. Colour therapy, or chromotherapy, has a stack of research behind it that shows how colours in our everyday lives can energize us, improve our mood, or help us focus, while others may be more calming and soothing.[22] For example, if you want to communicate energy and passion in the day ahead, ensure you wear an item of red clothing. If you want to concentrate and focus deeply, add a dash of blue. If harmony is your goal, go for some green, for empathy pink, for grounding brown, for inspiration purple, for seniority and respect grey and silver, and so on. You don't have to dress from top to toe in the vibe of the colour you want to express that day, and that colour choice doesn't even have to be visible (it could be your underwear). What matters is that you know it's there and authentically expressing something of great value about or for you.

- You can also express your sense of self-worth through your choice of perfume or aftershave. It's so easy to wear the same body scent constantly. Just because you felt a scent resonated with you on one day, it doesn't mean it will every single day moving forward. Perhaps treat yourself to several different scent or spray choices, so there's always that element of mystery for both yourself and others? Again, do some of your own research on the psychological impact of perfume choices. It's utterly fascinating and perhaps this glimpse will whet your appetite. For example, the smell of lavender mixed with pumpkin pie was shown to increase arousal in men by 40 per cent! However, lavender can stand on its own — the flower's scent has been proven to relax and arouse at the same time, which is a wonderful way to set the mood. And for women, it's the scent of vanilla that can increase arousal.[23]
- Well-groomed hair is also a plus when it comes to feeling confident. One study showed that men with well-groomed facial hair earned more.[24]
- If you wear a uniform, imposing your individuality isn't as easy, but you still get to choose the colour and quality of your underwear. You still get to choose how clean and well pressed your uniform is, how you groom your hair and what body scent you wear. You still get to add touches of your own style.

Your clothes and hair style choices are always going to impact your confidence levels in some way, so don't judge yourself too harshly if you still rely on them to help you feel good about yourself. That's the case for the vast majority of us. And if you use make-up in the same way, again, be patient with yourself. Going make-up free is a bold and brave choice – and I truly believe if you consistently work through all the 22 power moves in this book, one day you'll experience how liberating and empowering it is to show yourself and others the authenticity behind the mask.

That may be a while away, though, and that's fine. For now, simply enjoy the journey, safe in the knowledge that you are getting closer to that goal inch by inch. Take small but steady steps with your wardrobe and make-up choices each morning, knowing they are edging you closer to your end game, which is to feel great whatever you are wearing, even if it's just your birthday suit!

POWER MOVE NUMBER 7: Through Your Nose

I'm going to assume you're dressed now and your motivation levels are growing and glowing. You probably feel ready to take a deep breath and launch into your action-focused day. But before you take that energizing deep breath, it's worth spending a few moments thinking about exactly how you're going to do this.

You've probably heard or read somewhere that taking deep breaths can be revitalizing, so perhaps you do this now and again whenever you feel stressed or want an extra burst of energy. But because breathing is something your body does automatically and without conscious effort on your part, you likely don't think much about *how* you breathe. Your breathing just happens, and you flow along with that. And when you get dressed in the morning, chances are it's with your mouth slightly open – meaning you're breathing through your mouth without even realizing you're doing this.

It wouldn't be an understatement to say that noticing how you breathe first thing in the morning, and whether you naturally tend to breathe mainly through your mouth or through your nose, can change your life. In most cases, it is considered healthier to ensure most of your breathing is through the nose rather than through the mouth. Nose breathing is more natural and helps your body effectively absorb the air you inhale. Some health experts believe that breathing correctly – that is through your nose, lightly and slowly – is the secret to better health and well-being and perhaps even longevity, as rapid shallow breathing could accelerate the ageing process. Despite this, it's estimated that as many as 50 per cent of us breathe through our mouths instead, in fast, shallow breaths.[25] This most typically happens in the morning when we wake up and it then becomes the dominant breathing pattern during the rest of the day. It's associated with several health issues as well as chronic bad breath, so not a great start to your or anyone's morning.

Nose versus Mouth

To risk stating the obvious, the two ways you can breathe (and live) are through your nose and through your mouth, because these body parts are connected to your throat, which sends oxygen to your lungs.

Your nose has the perfect design for healthy, efficient and energizing breathing. Every time you breathe in through your nose, this releases a vasodilator called nitric oxide, which can help expand your blood vessels and boost oxygen transportation all around your body. Your nose is also a humidifier, as it heats and moisturizes inhaled air, ensuring it reaches the optimum body temperature for the lungs. Last but by no means least, the little hairs in your nostrils act as filters, filtering out dust, foreign particles, pollen and allergens, so there's less chance these will enter your lungs.

Your nose is built perfectly for healthy breathing. Your mouth, on the other hand, is built to help you eat, drink and talk. It can multitask, of course, and help you breathe, too, but that isn't its primary function. It will step in to quite literally save your life if for any reason your nose is compromised by nasal congestion, nostril injury or constriction and you can't breathe through it. Yet if you don't have these health concerns, breathing through your mouth isn't optimum, as we've seen.

A dry mouth is the most noticeable sign that you may be breathing more frequently through your mouth than your nose without even realizing what you're doing. This is because the more you breathe through your mouth, the more your mouth loses moisture. A mouth that's dry is at increased risk of bad breath, tooth decay and gum inflammation. You'll also be inhaling unfiltered air, which increases the risk of inhaling foreign particles and developing asthma. Over time, dominant mouth breathing can also be the cause of snoring and even sleep apnoea, and there is some evidence to suggest it may cause jaw and mouth deformities.

Your nose is uniquely designed for breathing. And if you needed any more incentive to keep your mouth shut in the morning when you get ready for your day, here's a reminder of the holistic well-being advantages of nose breathing:

- increases energy boosting oxygen intake and circulation
- filters out toxins, lowering your risk of allergies and coughing
- humidifies inhaled hair, so it's the right temperature for your lungs
- boosts lung capacity
- slows down breathing
- eases stress and anxiety
- strengthens the diaphragm
- boosts immunity
- eases snoring and sleep apnoea
- supports the correct alignment of the teeth and mouth
- freshens the breath.[26]

You might want to write these points on a sticky note and put it on your bathroom mirror so you can see it when you get ready in the morning.

You are never too old to learn how to breathe in the most optimum way for your holistic wellbeing. Whether you suffer from a dry mouth, bad breath, snoring, or just want to improve your concentration and overall health and well-being, learning to breathe from your nose more often than through your mouth can change your life for the better.

Acting Out: Case Study

Wayne had experienced a few years of poor health – nothing extreme, but he felt as if he bounced from one virus to another and was always the first to catch any bug that was going around. Barely a week would go by without him sniffing or wheezing or complaining of a sore throat and feelings of exhaustion. He was a skilled hairdresser but his clients had started to desert him, never knowing if he'd be in the salon or off sick with yet another bug.

We met after one of my talks about the power of daily rituals to heal your life. Wayne was at a point in his life when he felt stuck in a rut of poor health and low energy, and he wanted to do something to about this. He told me that he was glad I was writing and talking more about the healing power of doing, as he had tried meditating and positive thinking but had not seen the results he hoped for. I suggested he talk to his doctor as well as seeking alternative advice about how to boost his immunity and energy levels.

However, I couldn't fail to notice that when Wayne was listening to my answers to his questions, he did so with his mouth open. I told him that I didn't want to appear rude as many of us naturally open our mouths when we're concentrating, but that he might benefit from looking into the health and immune-boosting benefits of nasal breathing. I could tell that he was a little taken aback and explained he had likely got into the habit of mouth breathing due to repeated bouts of nasal congestion in the previous mouths. I encouraged him to do some of his own research and give it a go. After all, breathing is free!

Six weeks later, I got an email from Wayne thanking me and saying that he had followed my advice and gone to a breath workshop the following day. In that workshop, he learned about the benefits of deep breathing and was encouraged to breathe slowly and deeply through his nostrils with the help of a tutor for 30 minutes. He said that after those 30 minutes he was drenched in sweat, even though the room in which the workshop took place wasn't hot. The sweating alarmed both the tutor and Wayne, but it didn't deter Wayne from practising his breathing exercises every day from then on.

Wayne hasn't had flu or a cold since, nor has he needed to take a day off work for fatigue, and the quality of his sleep has improved. As a busy hairdresser, he jokingly said that he can't promise to keep his mouth shut all the time – as his clients love to talk to him and he often loses himself in the conversations – but he consciously focuses on nose rather than mouth breathing as often as he can. He believes this practical shift has made all the difference to his general health and well-being.

TAKE ACTION NOW

On waking, your body naturally wants you to take in as much oxygen to boost your circulation after sleeping as possible, so this is when you're most likely to breathe through your mouth without even realizing that you're doing it. And, as what you do first thing typically sets the tone for the day ahead, if your brain gets the message on waking that this is the way you breathe naturally, chances are mouth breathing will become an unhelpful feature of your day, and, over time, your life.

It's time to take charge of your own breathing now and help your nostrils reclaim their rightful title as the guardians of your breath. If you've fallen into the habit of opening your mouth, especially when you are concentrating on specific activities, it's going to take a while to shift breathing gears. As with all the power moves, start small and don't expect instant results. Take your time, and every morning try the two breathing exercises that follow, as they'll help you switch to nasal breathing. First, let's do a quick breathing check right now . . .

- Is your mouth open or closed? If it's open, you are breathing through your mouth again, so close it. Now take a slow and deep breath in and then out using only your nostrils. Feels good, doesn't it, especially now you're better informed about the benefits of nose breathing?

Belly breathing

Also known as abdominal breathing, this involves taking slow, deep breaths through your nose for several minutes so that your belly fills with air. This practice is thought to increase oxygen circulation and slow down the heart rate, therefore easing stress ...

- Sit or stand and be mindful of your posture. (However, if you want, you can do this exercise lying down somewhere safe and comfortable.)
- Close your mouth.
- Place on hand on your stomach and the other over your heart.
- Inhale slowly and deeply through your nose, allowing your belly to fill with air. Your chest stays still.
- Exhale slowly through your nostrils while pursing your lips to allow for complete exhalation.
- Repeat.
- Practise for up to five minutes at a time, so that you will soon be able to perform belly breathing with ease in the morning.

A variation of this exercise which is great for improving concentration is to practise quick and forceful exhalations through your nose with normal inhalations. Keep the inhalations and exhalations the same length. Continue inhaling naturally and exhaling forcefully, and repeat. And during the day you can also do a few minutes of dedicated nose breathing without anyone noticing you're doing it. Simply imagine there's a feather under your nose: every time you breathe in and out, you blow that feather slightly away and then inhale it back toward your nose.

Alternate nostril breathing

This requires concentration and is believed to increase mindfulness and feelings of gratitude for the present moment. It also improves lung function, eases anxiety and reminds you of the power of your nostrils. And it's very simple.

- Sit or stand, being mindful of your posture.
- Place your right thumb on your right nostril, closing it.
- Inhale through your left nostril.
- Release your thumb from your right nostril.
- Place your right finger on your left nostril, closing it.
- Exhale through your right nostril.
- Inhale through your right nostril.
- Return your right thumb to your right nostril, closing it.
- Exhale through your left nostril . . .
- Repeat the above steps several times.

Warning: You may feel lightheaded when you perform these exercises for the first time. Start slowly. And if you suffer from any breathing issues, be sure to consult your doctor before focusing on nose-breathing techniques. It's also not advisable to practise nose breathing when you're exercising or out of breath, as this can put a strain on your heart. This power move is confined to how you breathe first thing and when not exercising. Mouth breathing may also be necessary when you have a cold or flu or are suffering from nasal congestion.

Performing nose breathing exercises like those recommended here for a few minutes first thing will help you become more conscious of how you're naturally breathing during the day. Regular nose breathing checks can help make sure your nostrils do the work that they were designed for and take the pressure off your overworked mouth and jaw.

Your nostrils are always eager to do the great job of breathing they were designed for. Don't let your open mouth stand in their way. You can instantly boost your focus and concentration, ease stress and save yourself from all the horrors of gum rot and bad breath – and maybe even give yourself an instant natural facelift – by doing something as simple as keeping your mouth shut more often.

Remember, you have two nostrils and one mouth for a reason.

POWER MOVE NUMBER 8: Tomorrow, Tomorrow

Ideally, by this stage you're starting to incorporate the previous seven power moves effortlessly into your "get ready for the day" routine and feeling some of the benefits. But your morning of motivational action doesn't stop there. One more power move is loudly calling your name and the earlier in the day you perform it, the better. Not only is it a super power move that could prove decisive, it's also something you've likely never thought about doing before, until now.

Does the following sound familiar? Your morning is well and truly underway. You've got dressed, perhaps had some breakfast and completed your usual morning routine. The business of your day ahead, whatever that may be, is about to commence. Understandably, as you prepare, your thoughts will focus mainly be on what you hope to achieve or what you plan to do or need to do in the coming hours. Your intention is all about the power of now, the present day and what you hope to achieve by the end of it.

Power Move Number 8 isn't going to ask you to stop thinking in terms of your daily targets or goals, but alongside that short-term perspective it wants you to think about the person you will be tomorrow morning when you wake up. It wants you to take the needs of your future self into account. For a few precious moments before your daily activities begin in earnest, you're going to switch your focus from what you'll accomplish today to who you'll be tomorrow! And you are going to do something rather special for the person that you'll be tomorrow. You're going to record a short voice message for them.

Our will power is strongest in the morning. There is research to prove this, but it's likely something you intuitively know anyway.[27,28] The morning brings with it a new dawn, a new day and new hope and renewed energy after (hopefully) a good night's sleep. But your will power is very much like muscle power. The more you exert it, the stronger it'll get, but it will get depleted as the day progresses.

In other words, the more hours pass in the day, the more fatigue and distractions will deplete the strength of the level of will power we had in the morning and the more we'll need to go to sleep to rediscover it again. That's why what we do in the morning matters so much. And the best way to ensure our will power sets the tone not just for our morning, but by extension the rest of the day, is to consider our future self.

You Do Future You

"Make today count" is a happy way to live, but it isn't as easy as it sounds. Chances are your mind will struggle to keep you grounded in the present moment. When we're distracted by the hustle and bustle of life, there may also be rumination and negative self-talk. If this sounds all too familiar, a therapy that has the backing of research and psychological experts might just be the best starting point for you to live your day on purpose.[29] And that therapy is future-selfing.

Future-selfing is about putting yourself in the shoes of your tomorrow-self – the person you'll wake up to be the following day or week, month or even year. It's not complicated. You simply ask yourself what your tomorrow-self deserves and then trust that your today-self will take small but steady steps toward achieving those goals. In short, it's about keeping promises to yourself. It means trusting in a wiser future version of yourself that's looking back at you today with pride.

When we think of our personality, most of us think about our past and believe that our identity is fixed. Few of us realize it's possible to change our personality over time.

Of course it is. Think about the person you were ten years ago and how different that person was from who you are today. What would you say now to that past version of yourself if you could travel back in time and wanted to motivate them? Thinking about this will help you understand the potential of future-selfing. It's about the person you aspire to be, and that person is already alive within you. All you need to do is let go of limiting past mindsets and actively choose to become your empowered and liberated future self.

Thinking about yourself and what you want to tick off your list of goals in five years' time or even a year is a tried-and-tested self-help technique you're likely familiar with. Perhaps you've even done it or written a letter to your future self at some point, but felt like a failure when the five years pass by and only one or two things have been ticked off that list. Long-term future-selfing can have the opposite impact to what's intended and feel disempowering rather than motivational.

Mentally time travelling that far ahead in the future can be overwhelming, but if you start small and ask yourself what you can do today that's a caring act for your future self, this will help you see clearly what in your life is currently pushing you forward and what's holding you back. It'll also energize your brain, as questions (rather than affirmations or statements) will start to determine the way your thoughts take shape. Questions are the catalyst and motivator. They also force your mind to focus on what you need to notice, seek out and do today to initiate change that positively impacts your future. Successful people focus their energy on "hows": questions give them direction, motivation, creativity and momentum to keeping going in the right direction.

In a nutshell, future-selfing means encouraging yourself to decide whether you are going to conform to your past and present identity, or ask yourself what active steps you can take today to become your future self. It's all about shifting your focus to the person you want to be, and that future version of yourself is simply your best self.

Acting Out: Case Study

My *Premonition Code* co-author, friend and colleague, neuroscientist Dr Julia Mossbridge, is at the cutting edge of future-selfing. Along with her team, she has created an online resource where you can record messages for your future self and then schedule them to be played back to you.[30] Julia told me the reason she has invested so much of her time and energy into supporting the creation of this time-travelling app – which is online and free to use for all subscribers – is because of the promising results from a research study conducted by herself and her team on the life-changing benefits of talking to your future self every day.[31]

This study suggests that practising time-travel narratives – lovingly connecting with internal representations of your past and future selves – increases overall well-being. With financial support from the Robert Wood Johnson Foundation, a team of scientists and creators has been working since early 2020 on an app called Time Machine. The app allows people to engage in "time travel therapy" by recording and listening to audio messages as if these were from their past selves and for their future selves. Talking to past versions of themselves proved therapeutic, but by far the most significant benefits were achieved through supporting people in feeling connected to a wise and loving future version of themselves.

In 2022, Julia's organization TiLT (The Institute of Love and Time) conducted an eight-week pilot programme in partnership with Cook County jail. The programme was designed to integrate unconditional love and future-forward positive wellness messages into the daily and weekly habits of fourteen men. They were asked to make recordings as if their future selves were speaking to them from a better place than now. Not only are the recordings (which you can listen to online) inspiring and filled with love, hope and respect, at the end of the programme there was a noticeable improvement in self-esteem and well-being for the participants involved.[32]

TAKE ACTION NOW

You can practise your own version of future-selfing as part of your morning routine. You may feel a little emotional during it, because listening to a motivational recording of your voice speaking to yourself can give you a very real sense that at the end of the day you are your own life coach. You're your own best friend. You have your own back. Within you is all the motivation, direction and power you need. You don't need to seek it out there. As you'll discover, it's already within you . . .

- Every morning, before you start your daily activities, ask yourself what you need to do to make your tomorrow-self proud or feel better in some way. What caring act can you do today for the person you will be tomorrow?
- Be sure to remind yourself, when you ask yourself this question, that positive change only happens when you commit to it, when you stop hoping for it to happen and start doing something practical to make it happen.
- Notice how this future-forward question changes your perspective immediately, and how it encourages you to care about the person you're becoming and influences your productivity and sense of accountability during the rest of the day.
- When you have asked yourself this question and reflected on your answer, it's time to transform your future-selfing work into a power move. Take action. Grab your phone or a journal and write or record a short message for your tomorrow-self to read or listen to. Talk to yourself as if your

future self is filled with self-belief and self-worth and has nothing but compassion for you and desire to see only the best in you. Here's an example, but be sure to personalize it every day and add something new:

Hello, I believe in you and am proud of who you are and all you have achieved. I know you are always doing your best and that if mistakes are made you will learn and grow wiser and stronger because of them. I trust that you will be kind to yourself today and focus on what truly matters.

- Knowing you will have to hold yourself accountable to your future self – living up to the expectations you've set yourself – you will find that you naturally take positive and proactive action. For example, you might decide to distance yourself a little from people who drain you emotionally. You might think before you speak more often. You might make healthier food and exercise choices. You might ensure you spend some healing alone time and practise other acts of self-care that make you feel empowered.
- The next morning (before you record another message for the following day) be sure to read or listen to the message you recorded yesterday. Notice how you feel when you read or hear your own voice from the past talking in an empowering and loving way to yourself.

Interestingly, studies show that when people think they are being observed they are more productive and perform better. This is called the Hawthorne effect.[33] Being watched or evaluated encourages people to raise their game. Well, you're always being watched. Your future self is right here, right now, observing you as you read or listen to this power move.

What are you waiting for? Go on – do something to impress yourself!

YOUR WEEK ONE ACTION CHECKPOINTS

This week you've been encouraged to do things first thing in the morning that will help you start your day on a high note. By now, you should be waking naturally with a dream or two on your mind and eager to skip into your new day with a glass of lemon water in hand. You should also be more aware of just how invigorating cold water and deep nose breathing can be, how your clothes choices can raise or lower your vibration and how what you do today creates your tomorrow.

Don't panic if you aren't there yet with everything. This isn't a race against time. It's all about discovering what power moves work best for you. So, keep practising. Every day is a new beginning.

And you also have another week of exciting power moves to enjoy. But before you launch into them, here's a brief overview of what you've discovered so far. You could pop a tick next to the power moves you've started to practise and that you feel confident about including in your morning routine, so you can keep track of your progress.

Power Move Number 1: Wake Up Naturally
Ditch your alarm clock.

Power Move Number 2: Scroll Your Dream Feed
Immediately write down your night visions on waking.

Power Move Number 3: Rise Up and Skip
Stretch on waking and take up space.

Power Move Number 4: Make Lemonade
Drink a glass of lemon water first thing.

Power Move Number 5: Chill Yourself
Let cold water wake you up.

Power Move Number 6: Worth Your Wear
Choose clothes and colours that raise your vibration.

Power Move Number 7: Through Your Nose
Limit mouth breathing and breathe through your nose
instead.

Power Move Number 8: Tomorrow, Tomorrow
Go on now, impress your tomorrow self.

WEEK TWO: REST ASSURED

Every day, you have two incredible windows of opportunity to transform your life for the better.

When your brain transitions from sleeping to waking in the morning and waking to sleeping in the evening, it enters a highly impressionable state. What you choose to do first and last thing imprints itself on your brain and becomes ingrained in it.

Week One covered the potential of the first 30 minutes or thereabouts after waking to set the motivational action-orientated tone for the day. Week Two will help you tap into the epic untapped potential of the last hour or so of your day before you go to sleep.

When was the last time you fell into bed feeling content? Perhaps it was when you had a good day or felt you'd made a difference in some way? Perhaps it was when you felt pleased with yourself for a job well done or an exam or test passed? Perhaps it was when you spent the day with people you love? All are perfectly valid reasons to rest well, but this week's power moves will show you that you don't have to have a specific reason to go to sleep on a high note. You can retire each day with the satisfied feeling that your life has purpose, and you've had the best day.

The four power moves in Week Two are designed to be performed after you've finished your daily routine. Just as what you do on waking is important for setting the tone for the hours ahead, what you do before you go to sleep is crucial for a refreshing night's sleep and for waking up in the right state of mind the next day.

Evening is typically the time of day when you'll be gently winding down and probably wanting to think and do less instead of more, which is reflected in the gentle nature of these power moves, and the fact there are only four to get your head and life around. They are simple but effective things you can do at the end of each day to ensure you always go to bed feeling satisfied. Make the following power moves a part of your evening routine and you can rest assured that when you wake up in the morning, it'll be with a renewed sense of gratitude, purpose and determination – the defining features of a great life.

POWER MOVE NUMBER 9: Eat, Write, Love

Food is such a powerful and essential self-help tool for improving the quality of life that we're going to start this week by focusing on it.

The chances are we rush through breakfast, grab a sandwich or a snack for lunch and keep ourselves going through the day with copious cups of coffee, tea and (hopefully) water. It's in the evening when we're most likely to cook or take more time to think about the food served up on our plate. That's why Power Move Number 9 is going to bring your attention to your diet and the role it plays in everything you think, say and do, by asking you to keep a written record of everything you eat. And for good reason.

Food is your fuel.

If you give a car the wrong kind of fuel or not enough fuel, it won't run. It's the same with your body and your mind. To live an action-packed life, you absolutely must eat right, not just now and again, but every single day. There are no exceptions here: a great life can't happen without a great diet supporting it in the background. After all, it's not easy to say we have an empowered life when we suffer from conditions such as obesity, diabetes, high blood pressure, cancer or other chronic illnesses linked to a poor diet.

Are you giving your body and brain what they need to function at their peak? If you aren't, you won't have the physical and mental energy to achieve the great things you want to do.

Eating is something most of us do several times a day, and every time we take a bite of something or other it's going to influence our mood, mindset and motivation, as well as our physical energy levels. That's why you urgently need to educate yourself about the nutrients you need for peak performance and optimum concentration levels. Then you need to monitor your diet accordingly and fix any deficiencies. The simplest and most effective way to do this is to keep a food diary to find out if your diet is a balanced and brain-boosting one and then learn to savour and properly digest your food.[1] Power Move Number 9 is going to ask you to become your own food writer.

Make Peace with Your Plate

Fast food can often feel like the easiest and least stressful option when life is busy.

Big mistake.

To return to the car metaphor I used earlier, eating fast food is equivalent to trying to save time by not buying fuel and then having to walk or run everywhere because your vehicle won't run.

If you're reading this and prefer to choose the instant gratification of a fast-food diet over the delayed gratification of a healthier and hopefully longer life, you're choosing once again to be the hare rather than the tortoise. It's a life-defining choice and you may not get a second chance to make it. I'm hopeful, though, that you'll take this opportunity to reflect on your diet and adjust it accordingly. I'm hoping you'll make one of the most self-empowering decisions of all: to eat and drink well.

In the West especially, fast food and processed high-sugar, high-fat food consumption is becoming common as people look for quick and cheap meal options. If you're young, you may be able to get away with an unhealthy diet, but there will be a time when it comes back quite literally to bite you. Study after study shows that a sugary, fast-food, processed diet along with alcohol will age you faster and weaken your immune system.[2] It will also increase your risk of poor health, chronic disease and premature death.

The problem is there's so much contradictory advice out there these days about what exactly constitutes a healthy diet that it can be hard to know where to start. Research keeps offering what seem like differing conclusions, whether they're about red wine, omega-3, protein intake, essential nutrients to beat certain diseases and so on. The best advice is to ignore all this and keep things simple by focusing on what you do eat.

That's why if you aren't sure whether your diet is healthy or not, Power Move Number 9: Eat, Write, Love is here to save the day. Just keep a food diary for as long as you need to increase your understanding of exactly how healthy your diet is. Every time you eat a meal or snack, simply write down in a blank journal or document what you've eaten. Then at the end of the day, review your food choices. How do they compare to the common-sense healthy eating guidelines listed below?

- If possible, avoid foods that are clearly unhealthy and high in fat and sugar, such as chips, sweets and cakes, or restrict yourself to only eating them now and again when you are out and about, but never at home.
- Avoid eating too much of one thing. Strike a balance between what you crave and what is good for your body and brain.
- Always follow the advice in Power Move Number 4 by drinking water first thing and keeping up your water intake during the day.
- Make sure you always eat something for breakfast. When you wake up, your blood sugar level will be low, and you'll need to replenish it so your brain and body get their fuel source and you can get things done.
- When you want to snack, opt for nuts, seeds and fresh fruit rather than chocolate and biscuits.
- Cut down on your sugar intake in both your drinks and food.

- Reduce your meat and dairy intake so you become a partial or complete vegetarian or vegan.
- Ensure your evening meal is cooked from scratch and includes a variety of different natural food colours to ensure you're getting a wide variety of nutrients.
- Eat your evening meal a few hours before you go to bed, so your body has time to digest it.
- Sit down to savour and digest your food with an attitude of gratitude and get into the habit of pausing or putting your knife and fork down between bites.
- Aim to get enough brain- and memory-boosting omega-3 fatty acids in the form of oily fish, like salmon or tuna, or ground nuts and seeds; and eat B-vitamins in the form of leafy green vegetables, bananas, oranges, nuts, legumes and wholegrains.
- Limit alcohol consumption to no more than a few drinks a week.
- Smoking is off the cards completely.
- Follow the 80/20 per cent rule with everything you eat and drink. That's 80 per cent healthy according to the guidelines above, allowing yourself 20 per cent for chocolate, cappuccinos, crisps and other unhealthy but enjoyable indulgences. Sadly, the devil does seem to have all the "good fun" food. As it's nigh on impossible to eat and drink healthily 100 per cent of the time, just be moderate in your consumption of everything.
- Maintain good oral hygiene with tooth brushing and flossing every morning and night and pay regular visits to your dentist. There is a proven link between poor dental health and gum disease and poor mental and physical health.

Acting Out: Case Study

Paul is a busy real estate developer in his early forties. When his company expanded overseas, the different time zones meant that he is constantly on call and under stress as a result. He loves his job but often feels like he's underachieving.

A year ago, his doctors advised Paul to take medication for his high blood pressure, as he started to suffer from fainting spells due to his working long hours. His doctors also suggested that he pay more attention to his diet, as this would help ease his high blood pressure and keep his weight down. When they asked him what he was eating, he struggled at first to remember and said he hadn't had time to eat right or even sit down to a home-cooked meal for years. They urged him to keep an honest food diary for a week.

When Paul started to keep a record of all the fast food, sugary snacks and drinks and microwave meals he consumed, he realized he wasn't on the right food track. The excuse he'd given himself was a lack of time, but now that his health was at serious risk and his waist size was rapidly increasing, he knew that he needed to make a change.

Working with his doctors, Paul changed his diet completely. He cut down dramatically on sugary, high-fat fast foods and replaced them with wholegrains, legumes and healthy protein sources. He also made a promise to himself to cook from scratch at least once a day to avoid his blood pressure increasing due to the intake of salt in the fast food he'd been eating.

After around two months of healthy eating, Paul had never felt so good. Today, he also doesn't feel like he is underachieving at his work anymore. Quite the opposite – he works better and faster. He's still dealing with contacts in multiple time zones and under constant pressure to deliver results, but this doesn't feel insurmountable anymore. He knows his limits and feels on top of things rather than overwhelmed by them.

TAKE ACTION NOW

Keeping a food diary will help you really become aware of the strong connection between your diet and your performance.

- Write down what you've eaten and drunk immediately after you've consumed it. Then, in the evening, review your food journal and think about how it may have helped or hindered your performance during the day.
- You are what you repeatedly do and one of the things you repeatedly do each day is eat, so from now on really take a moment before you eat or drink anything to think about what you're putting into your body. Remind yourself that food is fuel and if you fill up on poor quality fuel, you won't run efficiently. What you eat today determines how you will feel tomorrow.
- Choose your food wisely. As far as a calorie count is concerned, most of your calories should come from unprocessed high-fibre foods, such as vegetables, fruits, wholegrains, legumes, nuts and lean proteins. Hence the emphasis on cooking from scratch when you eat at home. This will also help you consume oils and dairy products sparingly and limit your consumption of the empty calories found in sugar, fatty and highly processed foods. Depending on your activity levels, adult women generally require under 2,400 calories a day and men around 3,000 a day, but find out what the optimum amount is for your weight and height. However, rather than worrying too much about calories when you eat, focus on getting the right nutrients and how healthy your diet makes you feel.
- When you have chosen only the best nutritional fuel, switch your focus from what you are eating to how you are eating it. This power move isn't just about eating and

writing down what you're eating, it's also about savouring and loving your food. Busy people live busy lives, but when it comes to eating, fast is never better. It takes a while for the stomach to register when it's full, so if you eat too fast you may have overeaten, which can lead to poor digestion, weight gain and fatigue. The solution is to slow right down when you eat. Put your knife and fork down between bites and mindfully savour each mouthful.

- One tip that works for me is to play some slow classical or relaxing music when I'm eating. The first movement of Beethoven's "Moonlight Sonata" is perfect, as is Satie's "Gnossienne No.1".

- Another tip to help you savour your food and digest it properly is to eat with gratitude. Take a beat to close your eyes and give sincere thanks either out loud or in your thoughts for what you're about to receive. Bring a sense of reverence back to your table and put your hands together or touch your heart when you do so. You can choose a traditional or spiritual food blessing or make up your own. It can be as simple as "bon appetite", "thank you" or drawn from the Zen blessing, "In this plate of food I see the entire universe supporting my existence." It doesn't matter what you say; it's the gratitude and respect behind it that counts. Your body is your temple, and you are making an offering that is as nutritious, nourishing and as good for you as possible.

- Once your diet is on track, you might want to consider fasting now and again for up to 24 hours, as research shows that is the optimum amount of time to fast for health reasons.[3] (In many religions, periods of fasting or cutting down on food are part of the devotional calendar and are believed to bring clarity of mind.) Make sure you stay well hydrated during your 24-hour fast, as it's food you're abstaining from, not water. You might just find that fasting for a day not only makes your body feel lighter and more energetic but breaks down shackles in your mind.

Warning: If you've never fasted before, do check with your doctor first that it is safe to do so.

Keeping a food journal will help you to eat mindfully rather than mindlessly, because just knowing you've got to write down everything will encourage you to be more careful with your dietary choices. It will deter you from overeating and make you think about whether you're really hungry or not, so it's also a great tool for weight management. In a nutshell, becoming your own food writer will help you to maintain a healthy diet, and your mind and body will love you for it.

POWER MOVE NUMBER 10: Cry Yourself a River

Over the years, as you get older and busier, you may find that you listen less often to music or that when you listen do to it, you're multitasking so it's background noise. Power Move Number 10 is going to ask you to reverse that trend by making music a key part of your evening routine. For the next three weeks at least, I want you to spend a few minutes each day listening to music and giving that music your sole attention. But not just any kind of music; it must be music that makes you cry or evokes an emotional response.

You're going to find your own "sad song" (or songs) and in the process feel better about yourself and your life. There are benefits to listening to upbeat music, too, but this power move will encourage you to seek out those happy tunes earlier in the day, and to reserve your evenings for music that makes you smile and cry at the same time. It may sound like a total contradiction, but allowing great music to carry you away on a wave of emotion is one of the most rejuvenating and refreshing things you can do for yourself. To quote the profound wisdom of Gandalf, the wizard in *The Lord of the Rings*, "Not all tears are an evil."

Listening to a sad song or piece of music can be remarkably cathartic. Research has shown that it can help us process any negative feelings we're clinging on to and thereby bring temporary relief.[4] Sad songs can often feel like a best friend or a support mechanism that's expressing or singing about what we're feeling or once felt. They create a safe place in which to feel vulnerable and express ourselves without feeling judged or exposed. In essence, a great sad song makes us feel that someone else out there understands us, as they're expressing through the music what we too feel. We no longer feel so alone, whether we're currently going through a painful phase in life, remembering a painful phase or thinking about the possibility of one.

This may be especially the case if we're someone who finds it hard to tell others what we're truly thinking and feeling, or if we struggle to share how we feel. Through a sad song, we can acknowledge those feelings and try to understand them ourselves; over time this may give us the courage to start expressing our feelings more readily with others. Everyone is different in their emotional styles, but wherever you are on the vulnerability scale, and how ever comfortable you are expressing how you feel to other people, listening to sad music is cathartic and healing, like a form of inner counselling.

Play A Sad Song to Make It Better

Many studies have shown how music therapy can ease stress, boost concentration, improve memory and ignite creativity.[5] Listening to any kind of music is a great stress-reliever. It gives us time out to regroup. Even better, it's been shown to boost brain function – the so-called Mozart effect.

Music unites both the creative and the logical parts of the brain. The logical part of our brain is busy trying to make sense of the notes, leaving the creative part free to do what it does best, which is to imagine and dream. For once, both parts of the brain aren't trying to cancel each other out. They're working together to help us enjoy the music – and whenever our creativity and our logic work together, the result is inner peace. Most of our anxiety and fear is caused by our imagination and our reason stifling each other. Every time we listen to music, we're giving our brain the therapy it needs.

Music is one of the simplest and most enjoyable ways to heal yourself from the inside out and the outside in. To help you feel its healing benefits, the best place to start is with a sad song. And remember, you don't have to be broken-hearted for sad songs to work their magic in your life. For example, Eric Clapton's "Tears in Heaven", penned as a tribute to his four-year-old son who tragically died, can speak to the heart of anyone, even if they're not bereaved. This is the power of a great sad song. It's a powerful trigger that can remind us of the fragility of life, both our own and those we love, encouraging us to make the most of every precious moment.

Not only are there psychological reasons why sad songs can make us feel better, there's also a biological reason. It seems that when we listen to an emotional song, it tricks our brain into thinking that we're experiencing something similar. The brain responds by releasing hormones to help us cope with that pain, but when the trauma doesn't occur those hormones are still there to calm our nerves and clear our mind.

In other words, having a good cry to a sad song or piece of music will make you feel better. Forget trying to analyse why. Just ensure your playlist has plenty of sad songs to bring you healing, clarity and to help keep you going strong. Then make time to listen to some of them each evening.

Acting Out: Case Study

Sonia, age 77, cares full time for her husband of 33 years. He suffers from dementia and there are good days and bad days. On the bad days, nothing comforts and strengthens her more than listening to great music, and there is one track that never fails to speak to her. That song is "Time to Say Goodbye".

The song was first introduced to her several years ago by Julia, a friend she grew close to at a dementia support group. At the time, Sonia's husband had just received his diagnosis, and she'd been reluctant to attend the support group initially, as a part of her still couldn't accept her situation. She was also determined to manage it herself. When she met Julia at the group, the two of them immediately got on and Sonia learned that Julia had recently made the decision to put her husband into a care home.

Julia told the group that listening to the song had really helped her cope with all the conflicting feelings she felt. The group leader played the song and there was not a dry eye in the room. Sonia dreaded the time when her husband's condition got to a point when she would be forced to make a similar decision.

As the years passed, Sonia knew that she would have to prepare herself, as her husband's condition was on a steady decline. Time and time again, she would listen to the song, and it became a symbol of undying hope for her. It evoked a roller coaster of unstoppable emotion and somehow always makes her feel stronger and better able to cope with the circumstances of her life. Above all, it helped her face the reality of her husband's terminal illness. In many ways, dementia had taken him away already, even though he was still with her each day. Her grieving process had already begun, but she no longer felt alone, as she knew that besides her friend Julia, many others had walked the same path.

Sonia knows that when she has to say goodbye to being her husband's carer either because he needs to go to a care home or because he has passed over, she will find the strength within her to remember and be grateful for the good times. Listening to "Time to Say Goodbye" will constantly remind her of that inner strength and also that she isn't alone – others understand what she is experiencing and feeling too.

TAKE ACTION NOW

Music has the power to express and connect you to your deepest emotions. This is why we can find healing, beauty and hope in the saddest and most tear-inducing moments of music. Take a deep breath and come this way. Find a sad song, and let it play . . .

- Nothing could be simpler and more therapeutic. To get started, simply think of a sad song or a piece of music that makes you feel deeply emotional. Then download it onto your phone or wherever you listen to music, and build up your own library of music that moves you.
- It doesn't really matter which song you choose, as long as it's one that speaks to you emotionally in some way. Here are some tried-and-tested suggestions for musical kick-starters:

  — **"Everybody Hurts" by REM:** this song acknowledges the pain and suffering that everyone will feel at some point in their life – and that it's okay to ask for support. The lyric "hold on" offers reassurance that you can always find a way to pull through and emerge stronger.
  — **"Nothing Compares 2 U" by Sinéad O'Connor:** the strings and sublime vocal performance of Sinéad O'Connor make this the sound of pure sorrow with weeping strings. It's music to cry for.
  — **"Someone Like You" by Adele:** this is a song that makes time stop, sharing the heart-breaking and relatable sorrow of losing someone special who got away.
  — **"Hallelujah" by Leonard Cohen:** in the famous recording by Jeff Buckley, it's tempting to interpret this song as an expression of joy and gratitude, but when you really listen it's more like a cry of pain and despair. It is about experiencing life as a journey of spiritual growth.
  — **"Bridge Over Troubled Water" by Simon & Garfunkel:** this is about comfort and support in tough times, while the "lay me down" refrain is about there always being a shoulder for us to cry on.

- **"Back to Black" by Amy Winehouse:** a song that explores the pain of a failed relationship. That refrain, which says that words are never enough to say goodbye and how saying goodbye can feel like a bereavement, expresses the heart-shattering sorrow of a breakup.

- Don't forget the power of musicals, either, with sad songs such as *Les Misérables*' "I Dreamed a Dream" and *Mama Mia*'s "The Winner Takes It All".
- If you prefer classical music and opera, just make sure it has a sombre vibe. I mentioned a couple of pieces earlier that I listen to. Here are a few more tear-jerking suggestions to get you started:

  - Rachmaninov, "Piano Concerto, No.2"
  - Tchaikovsky, "Finale" from *Swan Lake*
  - Elgar, "Nimrod" from *Enigma Variations*
  - Barber, "Adagio for Strings" from *String Quartet, Op.11*
  - Mozart, *Requiem*
  - Purcell, "Dido's Lament" from *Dido and Aeneas*
  - Puccini, "Sono andati" from *La Bohème*

- At some point during your evening routine, be sure to put on your headphones and listen to your favourite sad songs. Listen to the music for at least three to five minutes for the full healing and mood-boosting impact.
- Make sure the music is not played too loudly and try not to multitask when you listen. Give it your full attention. Let the music flow through you. Make this your moment of healing.

You'll be spoiled for choice when curating and updating your most miserable songs playlist!

In the same vein, while it's best to avoid screens before bed, watching movies and TV can also have a healing effect, especially if it's something with a tear-jerking sound track, like John Williams's score for the movie *Schindler's List* or the song "My Heart Will Go On" by Celine Dion in *Titanic*, which describes a love that lasts beyond death.

Now, although this power move has focused on sad songs as the best place to start when letting music back into your life, make sure at some point to strive for balance and create a happy songs playlist too, full of tunes that make you feel on top of the world. Suggestions include songs like "Don't Stop Me Now" by Queen, "Dancing Queen" by Abba, "Walking on Sunshine" by Katrina and the Waves or "This is Me" from the musical *The Greatest Showman*. The ideal time to play high-energy and motivation-boosting tracks is in the morning. Evenings are for mellower and more reflective times.

POWER MOVE NUMBER 11: Start Another Chapter

What if you knew that there was one simple and fun thing you could do for 15 minutes each evening that could dramatically increase the quality of your life? Even better, it requires no physical effort – you barely need to move a muscle when you do it. You would want to know what that thing was, wouldn't you? Well, Power Move Number 11 is going to explain it in no uncertain terms. I hope, moving forward, you'll never forget what a big deal it is, not just for your personal development but for successful interactions with others.

Studies show that when we read fiction, we activate our brain in ways that ignite empathy and imagination.[6] Empathy is a superpower that will help you understand yourself and others better, while imagination is the most powerful virtual reality machine on earth and the magical wand that brings ideas to life and makes the impossible, possible.

Imagination unleashes creativity, solves problems and allows us to think beyond the known and dream of new possibilities. It's the driving force behind innovation and progress, and inspires change. In the words of Einstein, "Imagination is more important than knowledge. For knowledge is limited, whereas imagination embraces the entire world, stimulating progress, giving birth to evolution."[7] Visionaries such as Einstein, Marie Curie, Steve Jobs and Mahatma Gandhi, to name but a few, as well as every great artist, musician, novelist and poet exemplify the deep impact that imagination can have on society.

So what are you waiting for? This evening before you go to sleep, whether you consider yourself a fiction reader or not, make sure you retire to bed with a novel, ideally one you can hold in your hands, or listen to an audio version. Books don't demand anything much of you except your time. They don't cost much and won't judge you by your cover. Becoming a bookworm, might just be the key to your personal empowerment. Read on . . .

Become a Bookworm

The chances are that your preferred way to relax before you go to sleep is to scroll through social media and newsfeeds on your phone or laptop or watch TV box sets, movies or other videos online. You can still make time for all that, but far better to do it earlier in the evening. Just before you fall asleep, the best way to wind down is to get stuck into a great book.

Reading is not just enriching and entertaining, it's good for us. Research shows it can boost our memory, vocabulary, memory and creativity.[8] It enhances connectivity in the brain. It is also relaxing and a way to learn new things. Knowledge is power and well-read people are often better prepared for life's challenges. Not to mention that reading is terrific fun. However intelligent and beautifully crafted TV shows and movies are, they can't beat the brain-boosting potential of reading a good book each night, or listening to an audio book if you want to rest your eyes.

Perhaps one of the greatest things becoming a bookworm can do for you, though, is that it can help you become more self-aware. Sometimes books can start a fire within us, or make us realize things that we hadn't before. Taking ourselves out of the equation and watching someone else (even a fictional character) face similar situations to ourselves can bring a fresh perspective. It can also boost our empathy for others.

In a study conducted by Kingston University, after being questioned about their preferences for books, TV and theatre, participants were tested on their social skills, including how much they considered other people's feelings and whether they helped others.[9] The study discovered that readers were most likely to act in kinder ways than those who preferred going to the theatre or watching TV. People who preferred TV came across as less empathetic.

Empathy is a superpower that we all have. It's the ability to listen to and understand and feel compassion for others. It starts with recognizing and understanding the power of our own emotions so we can recognize and understand the feelings and motivations of others. Empathy is about being in sync with someone else's emotions – it's a superpower that makes people feel seen and therefore plays a crucial role in our relationships and quality of life. It helps us liberate the best and highest version of ourselves and others. When we start seeing others – really seeing them – that's when trust happens and genuine relationships can flourish.

In the Zulu tribe, the word for hello is *Sawubona* which means "I see you" and the response is *Ngikhona* which means "I am here". It's not about showing pity but simply accepting the emotions of others as valid. It is not about doing their feeling for them or reading their mind, but simply understanding what they're going through.

There seems to be a deficit of empathy these days, but we can learn to cultivate it, and regular fiction reading – when we immerse ourselves in the characters and situations in a novel, imagining what they must feel like – is one of the best places to start.

As well as being more empathetic, fiction readers are typically more open-minded and willing to tolerate and respect perspectives different from their own. And if that isn't enough to persuade you to sit down with a novel, book readers may also make better lovers, as judging by dating sites, the evidence suggests that people with thoughtful reading lists or book choices might just get a better response!

Happy reading!

Acting Out: Case Study

Sam felt her life was in a downward spiral and that there was no one who supported or understood her. She was taking medication for depression following the pain of a broken heart, after her partner of seven years left her without explanation. Some days even getting out of bed felt like an ordeal for her and she often felt empty, lonely and numb inside. But then she started to read books again. Although in her teens she'd loved romantic novels, she began with crime novels first. In a bizarre way, they helped her see that her pain was nothing compared to the pain of the victims of crime. She wanted a distraction from her own situation.

After a few months of reading serial killer novels, Sam picked up a book by an author called Colleen Hoover that everybody seemed to be talking about. It was called *It Ends with Us* and was billed as a complex love story with an edge, so she took a deep breath and plunged in. She read the book in under a week and although she didn't feel it was the best-written novel she'd ever read, the book gave her hope that however dark things get relationship-wise, you can always start over again. It also made her think about her ex in a different light. She recognized abusive behaviour patterns that she hadn't been willing to admit to herself or anyone else before, because they were complicated and mixed with real love, like they are in *It Ends with Us.*

To cut a long story short, something in that book liberated her from her past feelings of failure concerning her relationship. It challenged her to learn lessons from it, rather than to be derailed by it, and to make sure that similar patterns didn't repeat themselves in any of her future relationships. It helped her understand how very important it is to become your own champion and to stand up for yourself, even when your heart is conflicted and broken. Best of all, the book taught her that hitting rock bottom wasn't the end she'd thought it was. It was where she needed to build solid foundations and discover her own strengths.

TAKE ACTION NOW

The ideal time to read your book is in bed, just before you go to sleep, as reading is a much better way to relax and unwind than watching a video, which can disrupt sleep.

- Set aside at least 15 to 30 minutes every evening to do some reading. It's a perfect way to unwind.
- Switch off your phone, get into bed or find somewhere you won't be disturbed, and lose yourself in a good book.
- If, at any point, you feel that you're wasting time on reading about things that aren't real or relevant to daily life, gently focus on the evidence that proves conclusively that reading can significantly improve brain function and boost empathy and creativity.
- Remember how much you probably enjoyed being read to before you went to sleep when you were a child? Even though you're older now and can read for yourself, your brain hasn't lost its appetite for a really absorbing bedtime story.
- Reading fiction is strongly advised just before going to sleep, rather than non-fiction. Immersing yourself in an alternative reality will not only help you unwind, it'll also invite your dreaming mind to send you creative problem-solving dreams. (Power Move Number 2 underlined the importance of an active dream life for your well-being.)
- If you prefer nonfiction and can't remember the last time you read a novel, don't make this your roadblock. Save your nonfiction reading for during the daytime. Reading nonfiction is a superb habit that can boost intelligence and insight. However, reserve your nights for stories and mysteries that will allow your imagination to run wild.
- There are millions of great reads out there, waiting for you to discover them. Seek out a genre – romance, crime,

science fiction or thriller, for example – that speaks to you and get reading. If you want a starting point, here are a few of my personal recommendations, but as my taste leans heavily toward much -loved classics, it's probably better to do some research yourself and find a book that you can lose yourself in.

- *Pride and Prejudice* by Jane Austen
- *Jane Eyre* by Charlotte Brontë
- *A Christmas Carol* by Charles Dickens
- *Lord of the Rings* by J R R Tolkien
- *The Alchemist* by Paulo Coelho
- *The Da Vinci Code* by Dan Brown
- *The Boy, the Mole, the Fox and the Horse* by Charlie Mackesy

- Some books will speak to you more than others and you may enjoy some more than others, too, but don't let a bad experience with one book deter you. Find another and keep on reading.
- Remember that if a book has resonated with you in some way, you can read it again and again. Indeed, the mark of a great book is that you'll often want to return to it and when you do reread it, you will gain new and deeper perspectives.
- You can also recommend it to others so they can experience its healing power, too. You can do this impersonally by leaving helpful reviews on websites like Goodreads, explaining why the book is a must-read, and you can also personally recommend it to people you know.

Fiction seems to have the most positive impact on our well-being, and you'll really be doing someone a favour if you recommend a title that you've enjoyed, because it can be hard to know where to start when we want to find a good book. These days, with the closure of many bookshops and libraries, physically browsing the bookshelves may soon become a thing of the past. So, a personal recommendation from a friend or acquaintance can be helpful.

However, it's probably not a good idea to buy someone a book unless you know them well, because they may feel obliged rather than excited to read it. People like to make their own choices, so bear that in mind when recommending books. Having said that, there is something very lovely and thoughtful in buying or receiving a book when you know someone has put a lot of thought into selecting or recommending it just for you.

Nonfiction books can be just as therapeutic as fiction, so don't feel you have to stick with fiction in your recommendations. Sometimes nonfiction books, especially those about personal growth and development, can be life-changing. There's a book out there these days to help with practically any personal challenge, and the chances are that if it's helped you, it could help others too. Indeed, recommending a self-help title when someone is going through a hard time can be a simple and kind way to support them.

So feel free to recommend this book to anyone you think might gain from it!

POWER MOVE NUMBER 12: Closing Time

What do you typically think about and do for the last 30 minutes or so before you go to sleep at night? A lot of us are creatures of habit, so it's highly likely that your routine is similar each night.

Perhaps you like to write a to-do list for tomorrow or perhaps you prefer to switch off and spend that time catching up with friends and family in person or online? You might enjoy monitoring your socials, watching the news or a talk show, or listening to a podcast. You might want to make love or chat to your partner or have a relaxing bath . . . While there's nothing inherently wrong with doing any of these mood-boosting things, Power Move Number 12 is going to ask you to do something infinitely more empowering. In the last 30 minutes or so of your day – ideally while you are sitting in your nightwear in bed – it's going to invite you to make sure you first adhere to Power Move Number 11 by reading for 15 to 20 minutes, and then to close your book and spend five to ten minutes journaling. Journaling at the close of the day is wonderful self-help step that will empower your life if you commit to doing it nightly for at least four weeks.

Many of us save all our creative energy for the online world or for updating our social media profile, but this power move will make it clear that it'd be far better for your personal growth to keep an offline journal that speaks the truth about your life and not what you think others will want to see or read. For a true sense of self, there are some things that should be kept sacred and personal to you and only you. If you share everything online, you run the risk of losing yourself in the expectations of others. You become a reed blown in the wind.

People with a strong sense of personal identity have a part of themselves that is always sacred and private, kept back just for them. They know and trust their own mind – and find their own mind fascinating. They don't need validation from others for everything they write, say or do. Every power move in this book is edging you toward this confident self-realization.

Journaling is deeply transformative, because it helps us learn about ourselves and whenever we learn we grow wiser. It's all about helping us pay attention to our inner world, which is always going to be our rock, our refuge and our safe place when the world around us appears to combust.

The Most Empowering Self-Help Book is Written by You

Journaling about what happens in your life, and how you feel about it, isn't just a way to keep a record; it's also a way to understand yourself better and keep track of your progress in all areas of your life. Research shows that journaling about our aspirations and future goals significantly increases our chances of achieving these, as we get to check in daily to see if what we did in the day is in line with our vision for ourselves.[10,11] It also seems that when we write something down, this focuses our concentration and feels more official. On some level, we're making a promise to ourselves, and the mark of a great person, remember, is that they always keep their word, not just to others but to themselves as well.

Other research suggests that journaling can ease stress and help us come to terms with difficult situations. Like listening to music, journaling is a whole-brain activity in which our analytical logical left brain focuses on keeping an accurate record and writing it down coherently, while our intuitive and creative right brain is trying to understand ourselves and others better as we write.[12] Journaling will give you an opportunity to reflect on what is or isn't working in your life, so you can make changes accordingly the next day.

It also offers you a chance to express and feel gratitude, and therefore end your day on the best possible note.

You don't have to be a skilled writer to keep a daily journal; just remember that this practice has been proven to improve clarity and perspective and to ease stress, as well help us reach our future goals. Sometimes we may not know what we really think or feel about things until we've read our own words. In a nutshell, journaling is a remarkably powerful personal-development tool and when combined with your morning and evening power moves, it can dramatically increase your holistic well-being as well as your success and happiness.

Acting Out: Case Study

Three years ago, Stacey felt that her life was in a rut. She felt exhausted and unhappy most days. She was overweight, living in a one-bedroom flat and had a job she hated. Her relationships never seemed to work out and she was taking prescription medication to help her deal with her feelings of sadness and alienation.

Knowing she couldn't carry on for much longer like this, Stacey turned to YouTube and started to watch a lot of motivational videos there from the likes of Mel Robbins and Tony Robbins. At first, she thought they were related but soon discovered that they weren't. They were two distinct life coaches. However, they did both share the same message of the importance of personal accountability, and one of the self-help tools that both endorsed was journaling. Indeed, Tony Robbins credited journaling with saving his life.

Tony Robbin's account of sitting on a bench one day with his journal and deciding that he'd had enough of feeling inadequate really spoke to Stacey. The circumstances he described mirrored her own, particularly living alone in a one-bedroom flat with no kitchen and having to wash his dishes in the bathtub. Seemingly overnight, Robbins changed his routines and the first thing he did was to start writing in a journal about all the things that he didn't want in his current life and all the things he did want. He then wrote down what his ideal life was going to be and gave himself time limits to achieve his goals, ranging from next week to 20 years. Of course, from that day on, Tony Robbins started to achieve the goals he journaled about and went onto become one of the world's most successful and impactful life coaches.

Stacey felt she had nothing to lose. She found a blank notebook and pen. For the next few hours, she lost track of time as she poured out her thoughts, feelings and dreams. She also wrote a list of her life goals and set herself deadlines to work toward. Every day, she returned to her journal to define what kind of person she wanted to become.

Three years later, even Stacey is shocked by just how many of those goals that she wrote down in her journal have come true. For example, her commitment to daily exercise has resulted in the weight loss she hoped for, and her decision to revamp her CV and go on training courses resulted in a new job, which in turn enabled her to move to better accommodation. Somehow, the act of just writing down her goals helped her to create the clarity and motivation she needed to transform her life in every way. Journaling proved to her that her daily actions were creating her life, not her emotions and thoughts, and this showed her that success is a disciplined and action-orientated choice she could make for herself every day.

TAKE ACTION NOW

You don't need to buy an expensive or fancy journal, unless you want to and have the funds to do so. You just need pen and paper. However, although old-fashioned pen and ink are preferred (as it's always best to stay away from screens before sleeping) you can also create a digital file for a journal that you update each night if you want. Just make sure the light from the screen is dimmed as much as possible so that it doesn't wake you up when you need to get sleepy. Remember, quality sleep – ideally around eight hours each night (although sleep needs differ from person to person) – is just as essential for your well-being as a healthy diet and exercise programme. Alternatively, you can always speak your thoughts into a voice recorder.

- To keep this power move as simple and as relaxing as possible when you journal before turning the lights out, focus only on the following three questions. (If you find you want to focus on other issues, that's fantastic as journaling is a powerful self-help tool, but save it for during the day.) For now, reflect and write about only the following:

1   What did I discover about myself and others today?
2   What can I do to make tomorrow even better?
3   What three things am I most grateful for today?

- You can write a few words in reply to each of these questions or you can write paragraphs. There's no right or wrong approach here and what you write doesn't have to make any sense or be beautifully crafted. No one is going to read your journal but you. It's your personal and private self-awareness and personal-growth tool, for your eyes only. There's no need to conform or perform here, or to be bright and upbeat. The real power of journaling lies in your absolute honesty with yourself. Explore any darkness within, as this will help you to better understand and release any emotions that you're struggling to deal with and enable you to learn from them.

- The only rule here is to focus your answers around these three questions. If you find it hard to write anything, it can help to refer to yourself in the third person rather than the first person. Indeed, this might be preferable as it'll help give you a more objective overview.
- The first question encourages you to grow in self-knowledge, which is the beginning of all wisdom. Resist the temptation to focus only on the positives here. Write down what angers you too. A study in Japan has found that writing down our reaction to a negative incident on a piece of paper helps release that anger, especially if we draw a line through it after we've written it down.[13] It also helps us to learn and grow from what isn't working and reminds us that life is all about getting the most out of the journey, rather than being fixated on the destination.
- The second question encourages you to write down and anticipate or visualize what you hope to achieve the next day at a time when your brain is unwinding. This alert but relaxed state is the ideal time to plant suggestions that will take hold. Your brain is rather like the algorithm on your news feed: what you constantly turn your attention to is what then appears.
- The final question, arguably the most powerful of the three, encourages you to drift off to sleep with gratitude on your mind. Science shows that being grateful can help us to achieve our goals, because when we focus on what we're thankful for, we then focus our energy on what we do want rather than on what we don't.[14] Like often attracts like in daily life. It's virtually impossible to feel negative when we're feeling grateful. Moreover, a grateful mindset is also a creative one, as it encourages us to spot the opportunities instead of concentrating on the roadblocks.
- Simply write down in your journal what you're thankful for in your life right now. Start with the words, "I am

grateful for . . ." The "I am" is important as it reminds you that this time is your time. You're alone with your thoughts, and you can choose both your thoughts and your perspective. You are the master of what happens in your mind.

- The reason you should aim to write down three things is because one study showed that writing down three things for a period of two weeks significantly eased feelings of depression among the study volunteers, but the number three is not written in stone. You can focus on just one thing to be grateful for at first.[15] The important thing is that your thoughts before sleep drift toward appreciation.

There is always something to appreciate, however tough life is. We often take for granted things like our health, or the people or animals that love us, or even the fact that the sun rises each morning, and the moon comes out at night. It doesn't have to be big things. You can feel grateful for the chocolate on your cappuccino, as well as the fact that that you're still breathing. Practising gratitude is not about toxic positivity – denying or repressing negative emotions – it's simply about counting your blessings.

As you rest your head on your pillow and peacefully drift off to sleep, allow this appreciative attitude for what you have to carry you toward the infinite possibilities of your nocturnal dreams, rather than regrets for what you lack. Then, when you wake up the next morning, it will be in the best and most life-enhancing way – with wild dreams and infinite gratitude on your mind.

YOUR WEEK TWO ACTION CHECKPOINTS

Congratulations on completing Week Two. The fact that you've reached this point shows you're now deeply committed to acting first and last thing in ways that empower your day. Ideally, by this stage you're winding down each day with a beautiful recipe of music and books and gratitude.

To get the most out of the next thrilling week of power moves it is important that you carry on with your morning and evening power moves. Don't look back. You are on your way now. But before you plunge into power moves to liven up your day you might want to pause a little to reinforce what you have learned so far this week. So, here is an overview of what you have done this week to help keep you on the right track.

Power Move Number 9: Eat, Write, Love
Keep a food diary and savour every mouthful.

Power Move Number 10: Cry Yourself a River
Listen to a sad song or two.

Power Move Number 11: Start Another Chapter
Read, read, read novels that you love.

Power Move Number 12: Closing Time
Write down what you are discovering about yourself and what you love.

WEEK THREE: DAILY RE/ ACTIONS

Hopefully, the power moves in Weeks One and Two have helped you to understand the importance of choosing to do things that maximize your potential by giving yourself the best launch into your day with a landing pad afterwards. Congratulations for taking them on board. You're well on your way!

Don't get stressed out if you don't always remember to do all the power moves; even if you just do one or a couple of them each morning and evening, moving forward, you'll already be changing your life for the better.

While your will power is strongest in the morning and you'll likely be most receptive to suggestion during the evening, it's during the rest of the day that you get to act out, walk your talk and showcase who you are. It won't have escaped your attention that the power moves so far are all about you doing you. Helping you to understand that positive change starts with you and only you. You need to change yourself before changing the world.

The focus this week remains first and foremost on amazing you and on keeping that inner empowerment theme going strong. It begins with a power move that will help you consolidate all that you've experienced so far. However, as the week progresses, you'll notice that the power moves begin to lean toward empowering your interactions with the outside world as well. They consider the impact your actions are going to make on those around you and how what you do impacts them.

It feels wonderful, doesn't it, when other people value your perspective and presence in their lives? When they don't take you for granted and appreciate you for who you are? When they treat you with the respect you deserve and don't overstep your boundaries. It feels incredible when life doesn't feel like such a battle and everything you feel, think and do starts to fall into place, not just in your relationships, but in all areas of your life . . .

If you fully implement the following nine power moves slowly and steadily in your life and keep repeating them every day, you will move ever closer to feeling that your relationships and your life are in the right place. Great things take time to create, so you'll need to be patient, but the sooner you start living and acting the daily re/actions outlined this week, the better. As with Weeks One and Two, aim to add one or two power moves into your life each day, so that by the end of the week you'll have all of them working together.

In the knowledge that your future self is rooting for you to take decisive action today, and if you want to know how to walk your talk and feel like you really could sing out loud with conviction "It's a wonderful life" every single day, please read on . . .

POWER MOVE NUMBER 13: Walk, No Talk

How do you feel when people wish you a good morning, evening or day? Do you think they're just being polite? Do they truly wish you well? Are they talking about the weather? Have they had a good morning? Is it really a good day?

If these kinds of questioning thoughts run through your mind whenever someone innocently wishes you well, it's because you know deep down that for your day to feel authentically good, you need much more than words or wishes. You need to feel genuinely motivated, energized and empowered. You need to be the one to set the positive tone and the pace – not just be wished well by someone else.

You get to sleep with yourself every night and wake up with yourself each morning. Week Three drills down on reminding you again and again that life doesn't happen to you. It happens for you. In other words, you're the one with the power to make yourself feel great, regardless of what happens to you or what other people say and do. When life gets busy, or you feel anxious and overwhelmed, it can be so easy to lose a sense of your inner strength and to give your power away to other people and the whims of external outcomes. But if you repeatedly practise the power moves outlined in these pages, they will help you know for sure that every moment can be a good one.

To create a genuinely positive mindset no matter what, perhaps the best possible place to start and the best action to take is quite literally to take a step away. Power Move Number 13 is going to ask you to do the simplest and most natural thing in the world and one you've likely often done before, only this time you will understand its value. Ensure at some point in your day – ideally mid-morning – that you take a solo 20- to 30-minute walk outside in the fresh air. But when you take that solo walk you're not going to multitask or be wearing head or earphones.

Brace yourself. You're now going to commit to going for a silent walk outside ideally each day when it is light, or at least three times a week, weather permitting.

You will take a walk by yourself, without any talk. How does that make you feel?

Silent Walking

Have you ever sat on a plane or train and felt a sense of dread because you forgot your headphones and can't tune out the world without them? You might think that headphones keep you focused on what is meaningful to you, as you get to choose the content you listen to, but the opposite is true. Headphones are distracting you from your ability to direct your mind and your day. Instead, a steady routine of silent walking each day will give you a tremendous sense of personal motivation and direction.[1]

Still not convinced? You aren't alone there.

Silent walking involves going for a stroll, yes, but it's when you walk without ear or headphones or any other audio distractions. For many people these days, especially the younger generation, that may seem like a revolutionary concept. While it may seem blindingly obvious that silent walking can make us feel more present and help us focus, the fact that for some people it may feel like a "new" concept is a sign of how usual it's become for most of us to be constantly distracted from our own thoughts. To be distracted from ourselves.

Listening to music, a podcast or the news while doing our chores, going for a walk or travelling anywhere can feel like a great way to multitask. Although technology and phones have helped make our lives so much easier and more entertaining, the downside is that we never get a chance to experience "boredom" and the joys of a wandering mind, which is when brainstorming and creative connections can happen. In short, most of us today don't switch off. There's always something else to listen to and to distract us. In fact, some people never switch off at all and are quite literally distracted from their own thoughts and creativity. Instead, they rely on background noise and constant audio stimulation as fuel to keep them moving along throughout their day.

Of course, if you're out and about and find external stimulation difficult to cope with, then listening to music or a podcast can have a calming effect. Much depends on how sensitive you are to your environment. If you're highly sensitive, you will naturally seek out quiet time anyway. But if you use background noise to avoid challenging yourself with your own thoughts, that is only going to make any problems and challenges you face in your daily life even harder to deal with.

Surveys indicate that anxiety rates in young adults are continuing to rise.[2] However, silent walking could be an action-focused way to ease those anxiety rates dramatically, not just among younger people, but for people of all ages. With technology and phones taking over our lives and, in some cases, threatening our mental health, we could all do with a reminder of the importance of knowing we don't need to depend on digital devices like crutches. Anytime there is dependence on something or someone for our emotional and psychological well-being, this is potentially damaging to our self-esteem. Lack of self-worth and personal greatness cannot co-exist comfortably.

This book is dedicated to empowering you, 24/7, to take actions that will help you become a bold force in your own right. Each new power move takes you another small step closer to a place and time when you no longer need or want to give your power away to other people's expectations and to external distractions. You set the focus, pace and direction of your own life. Power Move Number 13 takes you out into the light of day and demands that you start making things happen. If you can walk without talk for 20 to 30 minutes and enjoy processing the originality of your thoughts and feelings while doing so, your destiny is personal greatness.

Acting Out: Case Study

Melissa, a meditation and mindfulness teacher, told me that ever since her partner's father had died one year into their relationship, her boyfriend, Carl, quite literally fell asleep each night with his earphones in. He couldn't exist without them, and she didn't say anything about it for months because she knew he was finding his own way to deal with his grief.

Things came to a head during their two-year anniversary, when Melissa booked an expensive restaurant and theatre trip to celebrate. During the meal and theatre trip, Carl repeatedly slipped his earphones in and when they got home afterwards Melissa gave him an ultimatum. If he wasn't going to limit his use of them and be present while he was with her, she couldn't see they had a future together. Carl was genuinely shocked, as he didn't think he'd been doing anything wrong. It was just how he'd got used to behaving. Keen to prove to Melissa that their relationship mattered, he promised to limit his use and go on an Airpod-free date with her the next day.

Melissa knew that Carl was a high-energy person and that meditation wouldn't resonate with him, so before she agreed to another date, she challenged him to go for a 30-minute silent walk the next day alone – without his Airpods. When he came back after the walk, he looked a little stunned.

Melissa asked Carl how it had made him feel. He told her that the first ten minutes of it being, in his own words, "just me, myself and I" had felt chaotic. He craved his earphones and missed being able to concentrate on the sound. He also felt vulnerable and exposed as he walked down the high street, as if everybody was looking at him. But then, after about fifteen minutes, the thought jumble suddenly stopped and his thinking calmed down. Even though he was walking in a busy high street, he felt quiet. He started to hear his own thoughts and ideas, and it felt inspiring. He thought a lot about his dad and his thoughts were happy, not sad. Indeed, he had so many thoughts and feelings that he wished he'd brought a notebook to write them down.

TAKE ACTION NOW

Set aside at least 20 minutes to walk outside without any audio or phone distractions. Mid-morning is the ideal time if possible, because as well as the benefits of silent walking, you'll be getting a dose of natural daylight at the optimum time to reset your body's inner sleep clock. Light is an essential cue for your body's sleep rhythm, and the light you're exposed to during the day will help your body sense when it's time for you to go to bed and to wake up. Remember that a quality night's sleep is essential for your body and brain to rejuvenate and for your day to be filled with energy and vitality. You need a nightly prescription from Dr Sleep, alongside a complementary consultation with Professor Dream.

Although you'll be gently exercising when you do your silent walking, exercise isn't the primary reason for embracing this power move. Daily exercise is, of course, essential for our health and well-being, and I could easily (and perhaps lazily on my part) have suggested a power move recommending at least 30 minutes of exercise a day, during which you should get slightly out of breath, or short five- to ten-minute microbursts of exercise several times day. Exercise has been proven to be as effective in boosting mood and motivation levels, and as essential for our well-being as a balanced diet and quality sleep.[3]

But this book assumes you've a healthy dose of common sense, already know about the life-changing benefits of exercise and that you find your own ways to incorporate it into your day. That's why the primary reason for today's power move is for you to focus clearly on your sense of self and to give space to your own thoughts and feelings, rather than those imprinted on you by your headphones, so that they take centre stage in your life where they belong. It's about motivating you to put an end to the normalization of being distracted from your own sense of self.

- To get the maximum benefit from silent walking, be sure to walk alone or with your dog if you have one. Always ensure that personal safety comes first when you decide to walk alone. Phones can be lifesavers in certain situations, so take your phone with you but switch it to silent mode. Choose areas that you know to be safe and if you have any concerns, walk silently with someone you trust but make sure that you both agree not to interact with each other.
- To get started, intentionally put your phone in your pocket on silent when you go for your mindful walk. That means no music, no texts, no podcasts. It will just be you taking you for a walk and the only sounds you'll hear will be the sounds of nature if you're lucky enough to live near a park or wood and/or traffic if you're in a built-up area. You may or may not hear your own footsteps, but you'll certainly hear the voice of your own thoughts.
- You could experience five or ten minutes of mind mayhem if exposure to technology, noise and socializing is your everyday reality, but please don't panic if you do. It's normal. Just keep on putting one mindful foot in front of the other. Indeed, you are practising an action-orientated form of meditation here. You are activating

and connecting to both your body and your mind and letting your mind wander. Don't try to interrupt those thoughts, just let them flow. If you find yourself noticing your external surroundings, just let that happen too. Curiosity is a virtue. When you're fully aware that you set the tone and the pace of what you notice and what you focus on, you can calmly observe the outside world and its interactions with your inner world at the same time.

This isn't to suggest that you shouldn't ever walk or run with your headphones again. Indeed, listening to music while working out can be very motivational and mood-boosting, but remember this power move isn't about exercise at all. It's a way to help you actively disconnect from distractions and make the empowered choice to consciously and lovingly connect with yourself – the place where all your true creativity, energy and power lies.

Should it be impossible for you to practise 20 minutes of silent walking for any reason, be it because of weather restrictions, schedule conflicts or physical limitations, you can still reap the benefits of ensuring that you get some quiet time to zero in on your own thoughts and feelings each day, free from noise and unplugged from technology and other distractions.

POWER MOVE NUMBER 14: Reputation Matters

You're close to the beating heart of this book now. This power move is going to make everything else in this book feel real. It's also the power move from which all the ones before and after it draw their transformative energy. It will motivate you to act today to ensure you're known as a person of good character.

I'm sure you have heard of the self-help art of not giving a f***. In short, this means not caring what others think and focusing on your own needs. There's a reason this advice has struck a chord in the mainstream, especially for those of us who are people pleasers, as self-worth should always be dependent on how we feel about ourselves. Indeed, reliance on others for validation is a recipe for low self-esteem, because it means we hand our power over to them.

However, for most of us our reputation will always matter to a certain degree.[4,5] This isn't necessarily a bad thing – if we're also aware that being respected by those around us isn't something we should chase, but which we should attract. It's a sign or marker that we're on track with our personal growth and becoming our best self. It is a truth universally untold that the people we attract in life tend to treat us the way we treat ourselves.

If you feel that often others look down on you, don't listen to, support or value you, chances are, you've unconsciously fallen into habits that don't just make you feel bad about yourself, they also affect how people treat and think about you. Power Move Number 14 will show you what actions you can take today to ensure your reputation, your legacy to the world, becomes and/or remains a good one.

You'll notice that this power move doesn't just focus on one recommendation; it groups together several personal integrity markers. They're small but powerful actions that you need to practise every day to save your reputation. And you will need to commit fully to them. In the wise words of Yoda from *Star Wars*, as far as Power Move Number 14 is concerned, you either "Do or do not. There is no try."

I Do, I Do, I Do

The following recommendations for empowered living will change how you feel about yourself and therefore how others treat you. If you want your reputation to be a fine one, read and do the following:

Don't be late: show up on time. If you have a meeting or need to be somewhere, make sure you're prompt. Rushing around while dreading being the last one to arrive is a drain on your own precious resources. The message it sends to other people is that your time matters more than theirs and that you're not on top of things, or that you simply don't care enough to plan ahead. Is that the tardy impression you want to make?

Stop gossiping: don't pull others down. Raise them up instead. It's very tempting to gossip, and, in some cases, gossiping can be a form of bonding, but if it's at the expense of someone else's reputation or based on unproven hearsay, it won't make you feel good about yourself. In addition, the person you're gossiping with may very reasonably wonder if you can be trusted with information. Gossiping makes you appear small, untrustworthy and unkind. Is that the reputation you want?

Cut out complaining: it's easy to fall into the habit of complaining about what's wrong with the world. Life isn't perfect and there are always going to be things that make us fume, but complaining about them doesn't change anything about them. All it does is drag you and others down. People will start to avoid you and the only ones who will gravitate toward you will be fellow complainers, as unhappy individuals feel comfortable around the unhappiness of others. What you focus on is what you tend to attract. If you aren't happy with something, stop complaining and start taking positive action to change what you don't like. If you can't change it, let it go. Be the calm and motivational change you want to see in the world. People are drawn to problem-solvers rather than problem-makers. Which one of those do you want to be known as?

Cut down your screen time: the importance of spending less time on your phone has been mentioned already as a way of developing personal empowerment, but it's also important when it comes to how others perceive you. If you're always checking your phone first, middle and last thing, the message you're sending others you interact with in real life is that the contents of your phone matter more to you than they do. If you're constantly hypnotized by your phone, others won't feel noticed, valued or respected by you. Once you consciously make the decision to check your phone less, you'll feel less stressed and distracted and more be able to focus on making real connections – and others will appreciate your undivided attention. Do you want to be known as someone who's absent or someone who is fully present?

Take responsibility for your mistakes: own up and apologize if need be. Hold yourself accountable. Tell the truth and if the truth hurts, be gentle when you share it. If you struggle to admit to your mistakes and always blame anything or anyone else, this is a sign of immaturity and dishonesty. It could mean you're not willing to learn and grow from your mistakes. Do you want others to think of you as a truth-teller or a liar?

Treat everyone the same: a mark of a great person is that they treat everyone with the same kindness and respect, especially those who are of no long-term personal benefit to them, such as waiting staff or strangers they encounter in the street. They don't save their best manners for those they want to impress or who can help them in some way. Their best manners are on display for everyone they interact with in their daily lives, from their barista to their CEO.

Keep your word: follow through on your promises and commitments. We've all said things that we later can't live up to, because life gets too busy or we forget or hope others forget, but that avoidance tactic stops from now on. If you become known as someone who makes empty promises or who doesn't follow through on commitments, you're showing others that you can't be relied on. Think about how you feel when someone says they'll do something but then doesn't. It's disappointing and makes you less likely to trust that person in the future. Don't be that person anymore. Do you want others to think that your word matters?

Respond earlier and faster: aim to do important tasks or respond to messages sooner rather than later, ideally in the morning before lunch. Stop putting off those things you need to do. Procrastination isn't the answer. And respond faster when people reach out to you for feedback or with requests. Don't keep other people waiting for a response from you for longer than is necessary. If a prompt response isn't possible, keep them informed about when they can expect a reply. There is nothing more disorientating or down right disrespectful to other people than not knowing if you'll ever respond. Do you want people to feel you are approachable or not?

Walk away when you are not valued: if you find yourself in a relationship or situation where your presence isn't valued, your contribution is ignored or minimized, or your voice isn't heard, the most empowering thing you can do is to walk away and never look back. Surround yourself with those who see, hear and value you.

Put all of the points listed here – or even just a few of them – together and you can see how they truly can enhance your reputation. For example, do you want to be forever known as the kind of person who is often late, gossips, is disorganized and negative, or the opposite?

The wonderful thing is that all the reputation-damaging habits mentioned here can be swiftly tackled. You just need to notice when you slip into them and then apply a little conscious effort to change. Change might not occur overnight, but it can happen if you understand the negative impact that certain behaviours can have on yourself and your reputation with others. Lasting change can happen when you stop trying and forgetting to do the right thing and simply start choosing to do better instead. Then, when you fully commit to consciously changing negative reactions into positive actions, you'll reap the rewards, as this will dramatically transform how others see you, and best of all, how you see yourself.

Acting Out: Case Study

Laura and Jessica had been best friends for over 30 years, since their primary school days. They spoke daily on the phone and met up as often as they could. Despite this apparent closeness, their relationship took a major hit when Laura made the decision not to ask Jessica to be her bridesmaid at her wedding. She asked her sister-in-law instead.

Jessica was heartbroken, as she had asked Laura to be bridesmaid at her own wedding. She assumed it was an unspoken promise that they would be bridesmaids for each other. When she asked for an explanation, Laura starting crying and said she'd wanted to ask her, but she couldn't trust her to be on time at the rehearsals or the wedding itself. She ran through all the times in recent years when they had organized to meet up and Jessica had sometimes been up to an hour late for no good reason. One of those occasions was Laura's mother's funeral six months earlier.

Initially, Laura had been understanding and patient and never complained, but when the occasional lateness became a pattern and even affected her mother's funeral, she felt resentful. Jessica asked why Laura hadn't said anything about this to her sooner. Laura told her that she had mentioned how inconvenient/upsetting it had been on numerous occasions via text or in conversations. Each time, she'd hoped Jessica would make amends, but the poor timekeeping continued.

Jessica was shocked to hear this, as she had been unaware of Laura's unhappiness and couldn't remember Laura trying to let her know. She just assumed Laura knew her life was busy and was happy to see her regardless. In other words, she had taken Laura's kindness and amenability for granted. Doing that had put an enormous strain on their relationship and only time will tell if their friendship can recover in the years ahead. The onus is now on Jessica to show, not tell, Laura how much she values her by keeping her word and managing her own timekeeping better.

TAKE ACTION NOW

Trying to incorporate all the good reputation builders listed here into your day can feel daunting, so the best way to act is to look through them all and see which one intuitively resonates with you. Some of the suggestions may not even apply to you, as you might have them in place already. If that is the case, congratulate yourself and keep up the good work. But for those reputation builders where you know work needs to be done, don't overthink it – just decide to do it and stick to doing it for at least a week. When you feel it becomes a natural choice or response, choose another reputation builder until you complete the entire reputation-building repertoire. And even when you can confidently say you embody them all you will still need to refresh and update your commitment to upholding them every now and again.

As you commit to living in accordance with your new values, please be patient and kind to yourself. A good reputation takes years to build, and everyone has different personal and social challenges to overcome. There are bound to be slip-ups along the way. When you mess up (and you will), catch yourself when you fall and double down on making a conscious choice to do better. A great life is not about being perfect but about learning and growing from mistakes and making progress in the right direction. Here are some practical steps that build on the points I made earlier to help you do exactly that:

- **Show up on time:** showing up on time proves to others that you are reliable, successful and in control. Moving forward, when you next have an appointment or need to be somewhere for professional or personal reasons, plan your journey or day ahead of time to ensure you'll be there when agreed. If you need to, set an alarm as your signal to get ready and aim to arrive at least 15 minutes early. Then, when you arrive, use that extra time to prepare and centre yourself. Notice how good it feels to be prompt and to arrive unflustered. Of course, sometimes life happens and there will be delays you have no control over. If that is the case, keep the person or people waiting for you informed.
- **Cut the gossip:** it's so tempting to join in when others gossip, but you can consciously choose not to. If the group excludes you because you're breaking ranks, that's a positive, as it shows they're not a positive force in your life. Be the person others can trust not to gossip,

spread unproven rumours or talk behind other people's backs. If what you're saying or hearing isn't necessary or helpful, step aside.

- **Don't be a moaner:** complaining is the easiest thing to do, but it's also the most draining, not just to you but to the person listening. If something bothers you, do something about it and if nothing can be done, let it go. Be the person who lifts the spirits of others and shares interesting and positive news. If you have nothing positive to say, keep your thoughts to yourself or fake a smile. This isn't denial or toxic positivity; it's about training your brain to focus on what's positive and not on what's negative. Faking a smile when negativity strikes is a great way to counteract it, because the physical action of smiling tricks your brain into thinking your mood is lifting.

- **Set boundaries for your phone use:** initiate a phone curfew in the evening, don't reach for your phone first thing in the morning and enjoy phone-free hours in your day, putting your phone away when you have meals and conversations with others so that they feel heard.

- **Stop shifting blame onto others:** take responsibility for your words and for your actions and the part you played in any disappointments, setbacks or mess-ups. This will feel uncomfortable at first, but the more you do it the more you'll feel liberated by it.

- **Be kind to everyone:** ensure that you treat everyone you encounter, whatever their role in your life, with the same level of respect and politeness. A good way to get a sense of a person is to watch how authentically they interact with people they're not trying to impress in any way.

- **Be more mindful of when you say "yes" moving forward:** practise saying "no" more often when appropriate, and when you do make a commitment, write it down and take it seriously. Put it in your diary and if you realize you can't deliver on your promises, let the other person know and explain why. Don't just hope they'll forget about it. When it comes to promises, it's always better to under-promise and over-deliver, rather than over-promise and under-deliver.

- **Tell the truth:** sounds simple, but if you tend to be a people pleaser, to exaggerate or bend the truth to your own reality, it's most definitely worth making a conscious effort to change, as nobody respects a liar deep down. The reality is that the more solid your reputation for honesty is, the more people will gravitate toward you as someone who is trustworthy, dependable and honest – a person of not just good but of fine character.

Imagine how differently you would feel about yourself and your life if you consistently applied all the reputation-builder suggestions listed here. It's not just about how others see you, but about becoming the best version of yourself. It's about attracting strong relationships, acting with integrity and being proud of yourself and what you've said and done each day.

Remember that slip-ups are okay – just catch yourself when your behaviour falls short and get back on track. You're slowly but surely taking actions that will rewire your brain. You're changing yourself and how others see you. And when you change in this empowering way, you will not only notice that others start to treat you with more respect but that they start to mirror you. Like always seeks like. Studies show that integrity and kindness are contagious.[6] By paying attention to your reputation, you're changing yourself, others and therefore the world itself one person at a time.

This really is your call to action. Make a conscious choice now to align your daily actions with your words and values.

Start thinking right now about the mark you want to leave on the world. You are the author of your own reputation and your journey to greatness starts with your next choice and your next action. From this moment on, make your reputation not just a good one but a great one.

POWER MOVE NUMBER 15: The Ears Have It

Walk Your Talk has focused on practical things you can do to help you feel great about yourself, from the moment you open your eyes in the morning to last thing at night. Keeping that feeling of personal empowerment going strong as the day progresses will radically change your life. However, for Power Move Number 15, the limelight is going to shift slightly to the impact that other people have on us, as well as the effect we have on them.

No matter how self-confident you are, there can be no denying that other people are going impact your mood and your behaviour through what they think, do and say. Loved ones are most likely to affect us, as humans are extremely receptive to the suggestions of people they trust, but even a brief encounter with a stranger can either boost or derail our mood during the day. Unconsciously we tend to alter our behaviour to match the expectations of others, and there's nothing inherently wrong with that. Human beings are social creatures who are inclined to place the needs of the group above their own – and that can be beneficial. But if fitting in feels like bondage, the key to breaking free is, of course, to become aware of it and to focus on the expectations you have for yourself. *Walk Your Talk* is your tour guide on that self-liberating path.

No one should determine your worth and importance apart from you, which is why the importance of self-focus and emotional detachment from the expectations of others is a theme that runs through this book. However, there is a surprising way that can help you to break free from the negative chains and expectations of others that you may not have considered before – and that's to empower them. One of the simplest and most effective ways to empower others is to be kind, and one of the kindest and important things you can to for others is simply to listen to them.[7]

Listen Up

Studies show that when people do something kind for others, feel-good chemicals are released in the brain and body.[8] This "helper's high" and the boost it gives our mood and self-esteem are experienced every time we do something considerate with no thought of personal reward, even if it's something we might consider insignificant, like holding a door open for someone else. It may sound contradictory, but helping others empowers us too, and can give us a sense of meaning and purpose. In short, it helps you help yourself.

And it gets better. Your helping others doesn't just empower them and yourself; it empowers anyone who see or hears about someone being helped, because it spurs them on to do something good for others as well. For example, if you witness someone giving up their seat to someone elderly on a train, this kind act restores your faith in the goodness of human nature and encourages you to do the same. Being kind is contagious, so in this way one kind deed can indeed make the world a better place.

People don't forget someone who has made them feel seen and heard. To paraphrase the late great writer Maya Angelou, people remember not what you said or did, but how what you said or did made them feel. If you make them feel better about themselves, chances are they will be more likely to want to help and support you too.

However, we shouldn't help people in expectation of a possible return. This power move should always come from the heart. We should simply help others because we're coming from a position of genuine self-empowerment.

A sure-fire sign of your own growing self-belief is that your unconscious or natural instinct is to lift others up too.

All things considered, helping others feel great about themselves is a win–win. Like seeks like and if you want to feel heard, try listening to others more. If you want support, try supporting others more, and so on. Try this "kindness to others first" back-to-front approach to your own personal empowerment for several weeks to see if it creates an empowering shift. You have nothing to lose but a little self-absorption. And the best way to start helping others straightaway is to give them your undivided attention when they say something to you. Listen to them when they speak, really listen.

Acting Out: Case Study

In 2019, when I launched my podcast, *White Shores*, onto all free podcast platforms, little did I realize what a learning curve it would be, as both a podcaster and as a human being. The podcast gathered a following, which was a dream come true and at the end of Season 1, I confidently invited my listeners to give me their honest, no-holds-barred feedback so I could plan for Season 2.

Here is a paraphrase of several similar messages I received:

Congratulations, Theresa, on an original and – dare I say it – quirky approach and a podcast that is refreshing in many ways. Your guest choices are outstanding and I love your sense of humour. My only complaint is that I'm not sure how aware you are of how often you interrupt [your guests] before they have finished making their point. I understand you are trying to make the conversation an interactive and spontaneous one, but I do feel listeners would benefit and learn a lot more about your guests and their perspectives if there was a little less interruption by you.

As a podcast host, hearing that your listeners want you to speak less and listen more was a rude awakening. You see, I'd always thought of myself as a great listener. Deeply empathetic. I was mortified that this wasn't the impression some of my listeners were getting. It was humbling. I was in denial at first, but when I listened back to numerous episodes as objectively as I could, I realized they had a point. My interruptions weren't deliberately rude and were often due to a genuine investment in the flow of the conversation or simple nerves, but when I put myself in my guest's shoes, I realized how frustrating it must have felt to them.

One of the reasons for speaking over my guests at the time was that whenever a relevant response or point came to my mind, I was worried that if I didn't say it immediately, I would forget it. I made the decision from then on – and this is something I should have had the common sense to do from the start – to have a pen and paper handy, so if something did come to mind, I could then make a hasty note and allow the guest to carry on speaking. I also realized on listening back to my early podcast interviews that I wasn't really hearing the answers that my guests gave to my questions. I tended to leap from one question to another unrelated question, as if getting through the questions planned on my list was more important than learning something from my guests' answers. From then on, I decided to ask just two or three main questions to kick-start the conversation and not to come to the interview with any more than that, so the guest had plenty of time to express themselves clearly.

In the podcast seasons that have followed, I've tried to implement conscious listening techniques and not to assume that because I was asking questions, that this was enough for my guests to feel heard or for my listeners and myself to learn something new. Since then, I've had appreciative messages from my listeners. I'm a work in progress, though, as we all are, so have a listen to my podcast yourself if you get a chance, and please do let me know if you feel I forget sometimes in my excitement that I have one mouth and two ears!

TAKE ACTION NOW

It really doesn't matter what your act of kindness is, as long as it makes someone else feel better or lightens their day in some way. However, if this advice sounds a bit vague and you want something more specific to implement right away, the greatest gift you can give others is to consciously listen to them. If you're pressed for time and can only manage to do one thing to help light someone else up, just listen, really listen when others speak.

The word "listen" contains the same letters as the word "silent". If you remain silent and absorb what someone else is saying, the gift you're giving them is your full attention and your empathy. Although conscious listening costs nothing, helping others feel noticed and heard is one of the greatest ways not just to empower people but to ease their pain. Empathy is not about agreeing; it's about understanding where someone else is coming from and seeing their perspective. The ability to empathize is what connects us as human beings. Empathy is evolution and the key to effective communication and conflict resolution.

- From now on, when you have a conversation, fully engage with your eyes, mind and heart. Don't fiddle with your phone or think ahead about your reply. Just give the speaker your undivided attention. Don't listen out for what you want to hear, or for what you feel is right or wrong, or wait for the moment you can interrupt to get your own point across; simply listen to understand where someone else is coming from.
- If you're tempted to interrupt, remind yourself that talking is repeating what you know, and listening is learning something new. To quote the spiritual teacher Ram Dass, "The quieter you become, the more you can

hear." When a person has finished speaking pause for two or three seconds of silent contemplation before you reply to show them you have heard them.

- When you reply, speak a little slower than you normally do. You can also paraphrase back to them what they've said, before giving your viewpoint. Try this approach and notice the spark of appreciation light up their eyes and the entire conversation. And on top of that, your no-rush, reflective attitude to conversation will be a sign to others that you're a person with gravitas.

- During the day, you might want to rate your own listening skills. Are you engaged or are your thoughts all over the place? Countless studies have shown that listening is a crucial skill for leadership and success in life!.[9] The sooner you master it the better.

- Conscious listening will have an empowering impact on others, as it makes them feel both heard and seen. It makes them feel good around you. Becoming a conscious listener involves looking for the gold at the end of the rainbow in what other people have to say. Your silence is golden and that is the great takeaway here. But this doesn't mean you must eat all your words. A conversation is a two-way process. Just make sure that when it's your opportunity to speak, you do so with an understanding of the other person's perspective and an awareness that your words have power. Make a point of using that person's name, as hearing their name spoken will feel validating. Watch your words. Speak your truth clearly. And if you know the truth is going to hurt, ensure it is presented in a tactful, helpful and not a demotivating way.

- In a world of fake news, alternative facts and the normalizing of lying, be the change in the world you want to see. Speak calmly and clearly. Mean what you say and say what you mean. Ensure your words and your actions always match. Honesty truly is the best and only policy when it comes to living a great life and leaving a lasting and inspiring impression on others.

- And when conscious listening becomes your default, make a conscious promise to yourself to choose to help other people in your life feel more inspired and empowered in other ways from now on as often as possible. This doesn't just apply to the people you're close to, but strangers too. Notice how good it feels to light others up. Remind yourself that you are not just benefiting them, you're also playing your part in making the world a better place, as kindness is catchy.

Warning: If you sometimes or often feel empty inside, your primary task must be to fill yourself up first, as you can't give from an empty cup. However, consciously listening when others speak to you doesn't have to feel draining. The only time lifting others up becomes toxic is if you're giving at the expense of your own happiness, or are in a relationship when you're doing all the giving. Giving to others should always be balanced with giving enough to yourself. There may be times in your life – when you're caring for someone vulnerable, for example – when you're expected to do all the giving. If that is the case, it's vital that you balance giving to others with giving to yourself as well.

If you want to help others, there can be no better place to start than to speak less and listen more. In our busy lives, we interrupt others without thinking, or lose concentration far more frequently than we realize. The issue with this is that it not only disrespects and disempowers the person we are talking to, or makes them feel that what they say isn't important enough, but we might also miss out on learning something new and important. Give people a piece of your heart rather than your mind, and your attention rather than your viewpoint. Notice how much you learn, how much more others are willing to share and how they change their behaviour around you.

While listening is a great starting point, you can decide to lift others up in other ways too. You could offer to do something generous, like regularly babysitting for a friend so they can have some time, or donating your clothes to charity, or it could be a small act of respect such as saying thank you to the barista who serves your coffee. It could be a smile when you hold the door open for someone or offering to help someone struggling with heavy bags.

Your small act of kindness is the sign of a big person.

POWER MOVE NUMBER 16: Fail Again

The goal of every self-help book is to offer tried-and-tested tools and techniques to help you live a happier and more successful life. But this book isn't like other self-help books out there, because in many ways it considers itself a last resort. It's the book you might turn to when all that positive thinking, meditating, manifesting, self-love therapy and so on just haven't yielded the results you hoped for. You're doing the "work" but still don't feel as empowered and liberated as you feel you should.

That's why the power moves up until this point have offered you practical and out-of-the-box ways to create a much-needed inner and outer shift toward living your best life – and Power Move Number 16 is no exception. However, in my humble opinion, especially when combined with the previous power moves, Number 16 is the power move most likely to prove to you and others that you're someone who should never ever be overlooked or discounted, whatever happens.

Power Move Number 16 focuses on how you deal with rejection, failure, setbacks and disappointments. Failure is your biggest opportunity to learn. The actions you take or don't take when you mess up or when your life sucks, or you feel that it sucks, will determine your character and your chances of future success and happiness, more than anything else. As failure is a precious opportunity for personal growth and where you get to transform pain into purpose, this power move is going to surprise you repeatedly. It's going to encourage you to dare to fail and/or be rejected and/or do at least one thing each day that scares you or makes you feel uncertain, rather than sure of yourself.

Surprise!

Get over it. Just like there are night and day, you're going to encounter both failure and success, rejection and acceptance, and fear and love in your life. Failure is an unavoidable part of the human experience. No point wasting your energy on complaining. That's life. There's no such thing as a 100 per cent successful and happy life.

Don't be fooled by people who appear to have it all, or who appear to be constantly "happy" and successful at everything; so often they'll have their own demons to fight behind the scenes too. They've just learned to hide them. Comparing yourself to others isn't a recipe for a great life. The only person you need to be comparing yourself with is the person you were yesterday. With that in mind, what do you think about yourself? Are you a strong person? Are you resilient?

If you aren't sure, think back to your last major disappointment personally or professionally. How did you handle it? If you were derailed by a personal disappointment, or you felt you could have handled it better, or it totally knocked your confidence, this is your chance now to prove to yourself and others that you're someone who walks their self-help talk – and the inspirational direction you are walking toward is always one of greatness. From now on, you're going to change your perspective on failure and see it as a stepping stone to success.

The road to success is paved with failure.[10,11] Think of someone famous who you admire and then read their life story. You'll find numerous examples of disappointment before success. I've already mentioned Thomas Edison and his failed lightbulb attempts, which he didn't describe as failures but as discovering 999 ways that didn't work, but there are countless other high-profile examples. For example, Walt Disney was fired from his first job for "lack of imagination", and Jeff Bezos had a number of failed online business ventures before he struck gold with Amazon. Another example is J K Rowling, the controversial *Harry Potter* author, who was rejected by all the major publishers and whose own agent said that she would never make money out of children's books. In all these cases, failure was simply a stepping stone to eventual success.

Without messing up, you wouldn't experience and learn anything about yourself, others or the world. Failure is your greatest teacher. If you learn from every failure and don't repeat the same mistakes, you will always be on the right track. It's not success that gives life meaning, but the journey toward it; it's the learning and acquiring of experience and wisdom that happens along the way that gives everything purpose and determines how you and others perceive you.

We also have this misguided notion that life should be fair – and that the meaning and purpose of life is to be happy all the time – but life isn't fair and if things were always smooth sailing, life wouldn't be the adventure that it is. Dare I say it, life would be rather dull. I'm going to quote the iconic opening words here from the million-selling, self-help classic *The Road Less Travelled* by Scott Peck: "Life is difficult." Peck goes on to explain that once we can understand and accept this great truth about life, we have a choice. We can moan and complain, and get stuck in our problems and pain, or we can find within ourselves the discipline to rise above and solve them. And it's the process of meeting and solving problems that gives our lives meaning and purpose.

Indeed, people born with a silver spoon in their mouths or who seem to never face problems should be pitied, because there is no personal growth. The actor Jim Carrey, a famous manifester who appears to have it all, but who has been open about his personal demons, summed this up perfectly when he said that he wished everybody could have all the money and successthey longed for, because it would show them that money and success aren't the answer to a happy life.

You may well think that sort of approach is all well and good, especially if you're a Hollywood star, but it hasn't helped you in the past, has it? The fact is you've now got to learn how to turn rejection into resilience and setbacks into lessons – and the way to do that is to make getting comfortable outside your comfort zone feel like second nature to you. That's why this power move encourages you to do small things each day that will make you feel uncertain, or which open you up to rejection, failure and disappointment, so that when the big dramas of life hit, and you face failure and disappointment for real, you'll have the resilience and strength of character not just to survive but to evolve from them and thrive.

In essence, your brain grows when you don't know. When you fail or mess up is when you're learning and growing the most. And learning and growing is the whole meaning and purpose of life.

Acting Out: Case Study

Doug was a hard-working accountant in his mid-forties, extremely logical and risk-averse. He owned his own house and lived comfortably. Career-wise, he felt totally satisfied as he enjoyed his work, but he believed he was unlucky in love.

From his early twenties onward, Doug had never had any problem attracting potential partners, but his relationships never seemed to get to the move-in-together stage. When I met Doug, I asked him why he felt that was the case and he shook his head. He told me that he really had no idea why, but in every case, he felt that he couldn't quite trust enough. He didn't want to invite someone to move in with him or invest in a relationship fully, because it might not work out. I told Doug that there was no such thing as 100 per cent certainty in life, especially where relationships are concerned, and that he needed to stop craving this.

To help Doug move forward, I asked him to think of something he would like to learn how to do but which would make him feel scared or vulnerable. Without hesitation, he told me that learning to fly a plane would be that thing. I encouraged him to do some research and find a flying school he felt comfortable and safe with, and to commit to taking at least three lessons. I wasn't sure Doug would take my advice, but I'm delighted to say that I heard from him a year later. Not only was he close to getting his personal pilot licence, but he was also engaged to be married. Stepping outside his comfort zone in his daily life had clearly helped him do the same with his heart.

TAKE ACTION NOW

Today and every day, aim to do one thing that isn't going to put you in harm's way, but which unsettles you a little or which puts you at serious risk of failing, being rejected or criticised in some way. In other words, something that makes you feel uncertain about your abilities to succeed and takes you out of your comfort zone. The aim is to help you become more resilient in the face of failure and to encourage you to learn and grow from it rather than shun it. You never know – you might inspire yourself and succeed, but, in many ways, it would be more helpful for your personal growth if you struggled a little before that happened. It's all about facing and understanding your fears, learning and growing from them and becoming a stronger, wiser and greater person in the process. Success, as wonderful as it feels, doesn't teach you a great deal about the kind of person you are or reveal your true character to others. It's easy to be a great person when things are always going your way. It's not so easy, but a mark of true greatness and strength of character, when they aren't.

- Write down the following sayings and quotes or commit them to memory before commencing this power move:
  "The road to success is paved with failure."
  "You fail so you can learn how to get back up again and grow stronger and wiser in the process."
  "If you can meet with Triumph and Disaster and treat those imposters just the same . . ." Rudyard Kipling, "If"

- Here follow some suggestions to help you experiment and test your boundaries daily. All the options listed here are designed to help you feel more settled when you're outside your comfort zone, the place where every great person can be found. Start small and choose one to perform today and build your courage forward from there. (Remember, though, that this practice is all about facing your own personal fears and some of the following suggestions may not unsettle you at all. If that's the case, find and face your own personal fears. It doesn't have to be doing something terrifying, such as a parachute jump. Sometimes the less obvious ways to face your fears can teach you the most about yourself as a person.)

  - **Post online:** do a status update explaining that you're going to step outside your comfort zone and ask your friends for ideas about what you could do.
  - **Shake up your playlist:** listen to music that you haven't heard before.
  - **Take yourself on a date:** go to the cinema by yourself or dine alone in a restaurant.
  - **Play the lottery:** you've probably told yourself hundreds of times that playing the lottery is pointless, as the odds are stacked so impossibly against winning – but this isn't about winning at all. It's about cultivating an

anything-is-possible mindset, and you-deserve-a-lucky-break-just-as-much-as-anyone-else mindset. It's taking a small risk, where failure is the most likely option, to encourage you to take more risks in other areas of your life. Also, whenever you buy a lottery ticket you usually contribute to a charity, so it's a win–win situation. And you never know – one day it might be you. If that is the case, please let me know. I promise not to ask for a percentage. I'd just love to hear your story.

- **Say hello to someone you haven't spoken to before:** speak to a person you haven't really engaged with before because they intimidate you; you might find out they've been trying to pluck up the courage to speak to you, too. (*Warning:* Be sensible and don't take risks by engaging with people who might endanger your personal safety.)
- **If you're single, ask someone out:** take a leap of faith and approach someone who catches your eye. At worst, they can only say no and if that's the case, at least you'll know where you stand. If you do have your heart broken, remember your heart is like a muscle: the more you use it, the stronger it gets.
- **Write a short poem:** there are no rights or wrongs when it comes to poetry. Stop telling yourself you're not creative and just do it. When you've written it, read it out loud and share it with others. Whatever their reaction, applaud yourself for having the courage to go there.
- **Wake up at 5am:** try waking up earlier than normal and use the extra time to do something you normally wouldn't – like read, meditate or sing.
- **Go wild swimming:** If it is safe and you are not putting yourself out of your depths as a swimmer, take a

plunge in the sea or a river.[12] And you might want to take that cold shower now, too, as recommended in Power Move Number 5, if you haven't done so already.

— **Watch a movie in a foreign language with subtitles:** this will offer you a new perspective and might just inspire you to learn a new language.

— **Change your routine in some way:** take a new route to work. Sit in a different chair for dinner. Use a different mug. The options are endless!

— **Take a physical leap out of your comfort zone:** take a trapeze lesson and then see what other new physical activities push your limits.

— **Observe a spider:** if you're frightened of spiders, take a deep breath and watch a documentary about them. Then, the next time you see one, take one step closer to it than you normally would.

— **Toss a coin and make a decision:** if you need to decide, for example, whether to stay in for the evening or go out, and simply can't make a decision, toss a coin to decide what to opt for, instead of stressing about it. Then take whatever action the coin demands.

— **Try new foods:** find a meal or restaurant you have never eaten or dined at before and give it a try. Wake up your palette.

— **Speak out:** public speaking is right up there among our greatest fears, but give it a try. Start small by giving a toast at a family reunion or speaking up more in meetings.

— **Take a nap:** if you think napping is only for the young and the elderly, think again. Try it. A 20-minute power nap, ideally in the mid-afternoon, has been shown to boost alertness and creativity.[13]

— **Incorporate power moves:** it goes without saying that working through this book encourages you to get out of your comfort zone, so add the power moves in this book to your day every day!

- There are countless ways to experiment in life and challenge yourself with new ways of doing things, so I'll leave thinking up more new things to do to you. A marker that you're truly making progress is when it becomes easier and easier for you to swap out the word "nervous" with the word "excitement". Go on, surprise yourself!

If there is one thing that great people have in common, it's their willingness to experiment and try something new. Yes, experimenting with new things brings with it the risk of failure and disappointment, but that's the only way to move forward. It's so easy to get comfortable with what we know we can do and what we know we like, but if we stay in a rut and keep repeating what's tried and tested, and don't venture further afield, we're at danger of getting a bit too comfortable and, dare I say it, complacent. Greatness and complacency are incompatible. Time to amaze yourself and others again and again and again.

The more you start seeking out what you haven't thought of before, or trying new things where you might not succeed, the more you'll challenge and expand yourself as a person. The closer to greatness you'll skip!

POWER MOVE NUMBER 17: Line in the Sand

"No" is perhaps one of the most seriously misunderstood words. When understood and used correctly, it has as much power to liberate you as the word "yes", perhaps even more so. It doesn't have to be synonymous with negativity and restriction. Quite the opposite: hearing yourself say it and then following through with clear boundary setting can be a reassuring sign of your integrity, self-awareness and inner strength.[14,15]

The problem is that "no" is often easier thought rather than said and done. This is because the human brain is hardwired to respond much faster and more intensely to negative than positive signals, perhaps for survival reasons. This might explain why you tend to focus on that single criticism posted on your status update rather than all the favourable ones. Studies have shown that negative information leads to a surge in cerebral cortex activity and criticism lingers longer than compliments.[16] This neurological over-reactivity may be one reason why we are often hesitant and reluctant to dish out negativity. We're aware on some level that it's going to cause damage, which is not a great way to win friends and influence people.

In a nutshell, "no" is tough, and when you hear yourself and others say it, this will likely make you feel uncertain about the stand you are taking, but the rewards in terms of integrity, self-confidence and personal empowerment are vast. A great starting point is to turn your thinking about the word "no" on its head, so Power Move Number 17 is going to help you do just that . . .

Flex Your No Power

We typically associate the word "yes" with positivity, courage, risk-taking and the like, and the word "no" with negativity, fear and limitation, but there are two sides to the coin.

If you say yes to everything, you risk becoming a people pleaser, gifting your energy and time to anyone and everything with an open heart. Say "yes" one too many times and not only will you lose a sense of self-worth, but you also risk burnout and/or experiencing the fallout of toxic positivity.

If you say no to everything, you risk becoming avoidant, uninspiring and an enthusiasm zapper. Say it one too many times and you risk getting stuck in a negative rut and, like the character Scrooge in *A Christmas Carol*, others will avoid you.

With both "yes" and "no", the attitude with which you use these powerful words is key. There is so much information already out there about the power of "yes" or a positive attitude (aka manifesting) that it doesn't need repeating here. However, there isn't enough emphasis yet on the self-affirming qualities of the word "no". Counting yourself out when something isn't a good option for you is also an important choice. It's about making the decision to put your own needs and values first. It's an act of self-care and self-respect.

It's impossible to have a clear and strong sense of self – and to understand that as a mature and responsible adult, you know your limits – if you repeatedly struggle to say no with confidence and can't set clear boundaries, not just with others but with yourself.

Indeed, the ability to say no to yourself whenever there is negative self-talk, or you need to self-govern, is key for success. But when does the power of "no" cross the line? When does saying no become selfish?

In general, the following guidelines should help you stay on the right side of "no". It's fine to say no:

- If you're asked to do something dishonest or that's not in line with your integrity or values. For example, if you're an animal lover, don't be persuaded to join a shooting weekend.
- If you're asked to do something that makes you feel uncomfortable or exploited. For example, if you're repeatedly asked to share your notes from a meeting that others could attend but can't be bothered to, you have the right to decline.
- If someone makes unnecessary demands on your time. For example, if they won't stop talking and demanding your attention when you need to be somewhere else, you must firmly let them know.
- If you are on a set course of action and suddenly realize you've made a mistake and fear the consequences of saying no, you need to deal with that fear and count yourself out.
- Similarly, if you are in a close and loving relationship with someone and fear their reaction if you set boundaries, it's more important than ever to flex your no muscle.

Start becoming more aware today and every day of what other people in your life are demanding of you, perhaps even requesting things that you wouldn't dream of asking yourself. Act now and draw a line with a clear and calm "no" and don't let energy vampires cross it anymore. Being generous and kind with your time and energy does have its rewards, but not if it gets to the point where others dictate your daily life, drain your energy and limit your own goals. Too many yeses and you give away your power to others. A few more noes and you feel in charge of yourself. You become your own boundary-setter and decider. You become a person others respect and know they can't mess with.

Acting Out: Case Study

Since high school, Ursula had always prided herself on being someone her close friends could count on. A shoulder to cry on whenever needed. When one of her friends broke up with her partner and asked Ursula if she could stay with her for a few days until she sorted herself out, Ursula didn't hesitate to let her stay in her spare room. And being the generous soul she was, as her friend didn't have a car of her own – having previously driven her ex's vehicle – she didn't hesitate to add her friend to her car insurance.

When a few days stretched into several months, Ursula couldn't pluck up the courage to ask her friend to leave, even though she really missed having her own space. To help her get used to saying "no", I encouraged Ursula to role play the conversation with me and to practise using the word "no" more often in her daily life generally, as I sensed she was someone that people often took advantage of. Ursula struggled to take on board this advice, but then life intervened on her behalf.

When Ursula's friend told her that she had racked up a speeding violation that would put her driving licence in danger and begged Ursula (who had no points on her licence) to say she had been driving, Ursula was finally able to put her "no power" into action. It was one step too far. This request crossed an ethical line for Ursula and before she knew it, she calmly and assertively told her friend that she was removing her from her car insurance, and she expected her to leave by the end of the month. Much to Ursula's delight, her friend knew that her time was up and moved out the following week.

TAKE ACTION NOW

Practising saying no to yourself, or rehearsing a refusal scenario ahead of time, can be an effective way to get more comfortable with saying no both to yourself, whenever a self-limiting impulse creeps in, and to others when they make unreasonable or unwelcome demands.

- Find somewhere where you can be alone. Stand in front of a mirror or switch on the camera of your phone so you can see yourself.

- Take a deep breath and say, "No, thank you" out loud, or, "Sorry everyone, count me out." Shake your head from side to side as you say this. How does it make you feel? What expression is on your face when you say it?
- Don't be surprised if you flinch a little when you first say and do this. The traditional "just say yes" self-help conditioning is strong. If you're superstitious, you may even feel as though saying no out loud is a bad omen, rather like walking under a ladder. After all, aren't negative words supposed to attract negative situations? Such concerns are valid, and this power move is in no way encouraging you to become negative and pessimistic, as like energy does seem to attract like energy. Instead, it's encouraging you to re-evaluate your understanding of the word and instead of thinking of it as a negative energy, to focus on its empowering benefits. As this power move has made clear, there are just as many benefits to becoming a "no" person as there are to becoming a "yes" person. It's just a matter of perspective.
- Continue to practise being a naysayer while you study your reflection and how at ease you are. Perhaps a firm and decisive smile at the end will help? If you have a history of people pleasing, this "just say no" mirror technique might be an exercise you need to repeat daily.
- As with every power move in this book, there's no point in doing it if you don't walk your self-talk. You need to exercise the power of no in your daily life. Now that you understand how important saying no is for your self-worth and for others to treat you with the respect you deserve, here are some common scenarios you are likely to encounter at some point. When you next encounter them, STOP, and don't let the power of your "no" slip away again.

  — A friend asks for your help one too many times, without returning any of those favours.

- The phone rings and it's a sales call for a product or service you don't need.
- An acquaintance you barely know (and don't want to know) keeps pestering you with unwanted calls.
- A colleague wants you to drop everything to give them immediate advice.
- Your partner or child always expects you to do the housework or cooking.
- You're asked by someone you care about to sign a petition about something you don't care about.
- You're invited to a party everyone is going to but have made other plans.
- Someone repeatedly tries to engage you in conversation when you'd prefer to be left alone.
- You've had enough to drink, but your best friend demands you have another.
- One of your friends asks if they can rent your holiday cottage to meet their lover. The only problem is that their lover is not their partner.

• Keep practising your polite "no power" every time you encounter the above scenarios and others like them. You aren't being selfish. You are taking personal responsibility. You are letting yourself and others know that while other people are important to you and you will be there for others when and if you can, sometimes you must draw your own line in the sand for your own well-being.

• If your instinct is to be generous and agreeable, this isn't a bad thing, it's a good thing, but you urgently need to toughen up before others take too many pieces of yourself away from you. When you want to say no but can't get the words out, a great starting point is to say, "I'll think about it", or, "Give me a few days and I'll let you know." This will soften the impact of your no when you do deliver it, while also giving you the opportunity to make sure your decision is a thoughtful one.

- Should you continue to struggle to roll the word no off your tongue with ease, try these alternatives until you get there:

  - "I'm not comfortable with that."
  - "Sorry, I would rather not."
  - "Let's agree to disagree."
  - "Thank you for asking me, but not on this occasion."

You're still saying no but in a gentler way. Try to ensure your refusal is delivered in a calm and non-emotional way. And resist the urge to offer endless explanations for your refusal. It is your right to say no.

Trust that when you commit to this power move and start feeling the strength of saying no to whatever isn't in your best interests, your inner worth will skyrocket. You will also notice that other people have less and less influence over you. It becomes easier to say no to negative personal habits, too, such as overeating, smoking and self-criticism, and it also becomes easier to say no to people who drain you or make you feel guilty. At the same time, without the power of yes, there would be no power of no – the two define each other just as day needs night – so it becomes so much easier to say yes to what's good for you. You'll start to share more of your life with people who give as much to you as you give to them.

And if you do find yourself being on the receiving end of a calm and clear no from someone else, you don't need to flinch or feel roadblocked anymore. You will know exactly where you stand with that person and what their own line in the sand is.

When you start flexing your no muscle more often, you may well find that others get offended and take issue or test your boundaries. That's the "don't take no for an answer" response that every salesperson is taught. If you encounter this sort of behaviour, it's more important than ever to stand your ground – to draw your line. Stick up for yourself. If you don't, nobody else will.

With your newfound knowledge of "no power", should you still feel that you can't say no, then you have to consider whether your relationships are genuine, or whether you're being controlled in them. The ability to say no when the occasion demands shows others what your moral compass is and what your character is. Are you a nice but malleable people pleaser or do you have personal integrity and a backbone?

We all succumb at times to saying or doing what we think others want to hear or see, or we go along with things because we want to be liked and considered a nice person. But why on earth would we ever want others to think of us as being "nice"? I don't know about you, but my teachers at school always urged me to avoid using the word "nice" in essays, because it's bland and boring . . . Everything that walking your talk is not!

POWER MOVE NUMBER 18: Get Rid

Forget the stereotype of the chaotic office or workspace of the genius professor, inventor or entrepreneur. Yes, they may function better when surrounded by mess, and Steve Jobs was apparently a case in point, but many of these people have a long-suffering assistant somewhere in the background who quietly helps brings some method to their seeming madness. While most of us can't afford the luxury of hired help, the truth is that unnecessary clutter induces stress. It slows us right down, messes with our goal setting and, quite rightly, give others the impression that we're a disorganized, sloppy and unreliable person. That we don't care enough to take proactive action either for others or for ourselves.

A big stride in the right direction when you want to change your life is to get your physical stuff organized.[17] There's a direct relationship between decluttering and feeling you are in control of your life.[18] Clutter is confusion and a metaphor for not being able to see the wood for the trees. In contrast, tidying up on the outside reinforces the importance of inner clarity, discipline and a life lived on purpose.

Power Move Number 18 demands that you get a handle on unnecessary clutter and not in a piecemeal, picky manner but in a radical way. No more putting it off. You are going to initiate today – and/or schedule in your diary – a time to set in motion a major declutter of your home, car and workspace. And from that reset point, you're going to keep the tidying momentum going strong every day. You aren't going back. Organized and decluttered living and working spaces are going to be your new normal.

Making sure that your home and working environment are clean, tidy and well organized is a big sign you respect yourself and any others that enter your space. Moreover, the act of tidying up really does have power to attract success into your life. It feels liberating when you do it and becomes a catalyst for wanting similar lightness and clarity in all areas of your life.

Do you want others to think of you as chaotic or commanding? Disorganized and directionless, or disciplined and focused? More importantly, do you want to think of yourself as flaky or focused? Assuming it's the latter, stock up now on those bin bags and read on . . .

The Power of Tidying Up

The stress hormone cortisol is released when we're surrounded by clutter and the disorder it brings.[19] Your health is going to benefit from a tidy-up, because it's well documented that stress is bad news physically, emotionally and mentally.

Clutter has also been shown to impact focus. One study set people the same task but separated them into groups. One group performed that task in an organized environment and the other group in a disorganized one.[20] There was marked lack of focus and a decrease in performance in the second group. Clutter distracts, so getting rid of it can increase our con-centration, focus and creativity. In addition, clutter appears to send a signal to our brain that our life is disorganized too, and this increases the likelihood of anxiety. And a less well-known benefit of tidying up is that it helps you relax and sleep better.

Many of us are guilty of clinging onto things for sentimental reasons, even items that have negative memories associated with them. And we all hang on to certain things, but if kept too long they can slow us down or make us feel guilty or that we failed; for example, that exercise bike we don't use but which is great for draping things over. Decluttering can give you a chance to clean up your life emotionally and let go of it all.

Acting Out: Case Study

Amanda felt a constant knot of tension in her stomach. Sometimes she found it painful, especially when she was eating and drinking. Worried that she might have some chronic undiagnosed illness, she consulted her doctor, who conducted tests but could find nothing seriously wrong. He suggested that her difficulty swallowing might be down to acid reflux and encouraged her to take medication and to practise stress-management techniques.

What Amanda didn't tell her doctor was that her marriage of 14 years was in crisis. There was no third party involved. She and her husband just didn't seem to make each other happy anymore. Amanda didn't want to give up on the relationship and suggested they have some time apart from each other to think. Her husband agreed and went to stay with his brother for a few weeks. Amanda found the silence at home alarming at first. So, to keep herself distracted, she decided this would be the optimum time to tidy up the house.

She started in the bedroom she shared with her husband. She had no idea how much forgotten junk, clothes, books and other things they had gathered over the years. It was easy for her to decide what she wanted to keep and throw out among her own items, but when it came to her husband's possessions, she felt nothing but panic. She could not decide for him so simply organized all his items into categories and placed them in the spare room for him to sort out when he came back.

Once her husband's things were out of the bedroom and she'd sorted through her own belongings, Amanda had a good night's sleep for the first time in months. And when she woke up in the morning that tight feeling in her stomach had eased. Rather than a period of reflection, the act of decluttering her bedroom had made it abundantly clear that she no longer needed or wanted her husband in her life either. It was time to let go of her marriage.

TAKE ACTION NOW

Tidy and well-organized living and work spaces will maximize your effectiveness and give you a sense of discipline and focus. Whenever we live surrounded by clutter, it's impossible to have clarity about what we're doing. Enough said – that unhealthy dynamic changes now. This is a seriously effective outside-in power move that is going to change the way you think and feel, because each time you let go of stuff that is cluttering up your life unnecessarily, you send a message to yourself that you need to let go of mindsets that no longer serve you either.

If you believe you haven't got time to organize a declutter or simply can't face it, choose to ditch those tired old excuses right now. Time spent decluttering will save you time in the long run. For example, if you tidy up each day, you won't waste time every morning trying to find your keys or other important items. You'll know exactly where they are. And if the whole idea still feels overwhelming, remind yourself that changing your life for the better *is* going to take effort on your part. There is no easy path to success. You either do or you don't. There is no try.

- Look at your diary and block out a day and time for a radical – not a piecemeal – declutter. Then, when the day and time come round, roll up your sleeves and get down to it. Only keep what you actively use or what brings you joy. Get rid of, or sell, the rest. If you can, donate it to charity.
- Be ruthless in your decluttering. According to Japanese decluttering queen Marie Kondo, author of the million-copy bestseller *The Life-Changing Magic of Tidying Up*, what you want to keep in your life is a symbol of how you want to live your life. Tidying up will help you see clearly

what you do and don't need. (And don't think storing things away is decluttering. It isn't, because you're still hanging on to it.)

- As you work through sorting and organizing your stuff, Kondo advises that you hold each item and ask yourself if it brings you happiness. If it does, keep it. If it doesn't, get rid. In the words of motivational speaker and author Jordan Peterson, "If you want to organize your psyche (mind), start by clearing up your room." By exercising some kind of control over your environment, you can put your life in order too. It's a dynamic example of the outside-in approach to personal growth.

- What we do impacts our brain, just as much as what we think impacts our actions. Every time you clear space, you create a dynamic energy shift, so clear out the old and welcome in the new. You might even want to play that empowering song from *Frozen*, "Let It Go", on a loop when you do your decluttering!

- Start with one room or cupboard at a time. Aim to sort it out once and for all. When you have finished, look at your diary and book a day and time for the next room or cupboard radical clear-out.

- Begin the tidying up by putting everything in heaps on the floor according to category. Start with clothes and shoes first, then papers and books, sentimental items and miscellany.

- Take each item and decide if it is something you use and need and/or if it brings you joy. If it doesn't tick either box, mentally thank it for its service and then put it in your bin bag. Be ruthless. It's just a thing, and you can't take it with you. The Egyptians tried that and their pyramids got robbed.

- Don't worry about where your discarded items will go until you're done discarding everything.

- When you have systematically gone through each room, drawer and cupboard, the focus turns to daily maintenance. Tidy up one thing each day, even if it's something as simple as emptying your pockets or sorting the pens on your desk.

- Making your bed each morning is a highly recommended act and symbol of self-discipline – and there's nothing more satisfying than flopping into a well-made bed at night.

- Organize and stick to a regular cleaning schedule. Keep track of new clutter. Only keep what you can use and/or find beautiful and life-enhancing.

- Make a conscious decision to keep a firm grip on the stuff that follows you into your living areas and work space – remember it's a striking metaphor for a lack of mental clarity and self-discipline. You're better than that.

- Remember that letting go doesn't have to be painful or traumatic. Every year, when leaves fall from autumn trees and light up the world with their colours, they teach us not just how necessary new beginnings are, but also how beautiful letting go can be.

- To experience the life-changing power of tidying up, you must think of it as a marathon and not a sprint. You can't declutter your home and life overnight; it's a constant work in progress.

- Take note in the coming days of any correlation you feel between your ability to focus, create and concentrate, and your radical declutter schedule. You'll probably be pleasantly surprised.

If you already know and practise the benefits of tidying up daily, congratulate yourself and stay on track. Let this power move inspire you to keep up the good work and be even more mindful of the reason you are doing it. This radical "get rid" mentality will filter slowly but surely into the rest of your life and empower you to let go of any relationships, habits, thought patterns and other unwanted emotional and mental clutter that may have served you well once, but no longer serves you now.

Controlling the clutter in your life is a great way to clear your mind, choose and control what you surround yourself with, or let into your life. Wherever there is clutter in your home or work place, there will be metaphorical clutter for you mentally, emotionally and physically. Consciously reminding yourself that you're not just doing an external clean-up, you're also getting rid of negative energy within yourself, can be a mighty powerful incentive.

POWER MOVE NUMBER 19: Look Up

Whether or not there is life after death (in terms of the survival of consciousness) is a subject of serious and ongoing debate, but one thing is becoming increasingly certain: when we die our digital footprint lingers on in the ether. In the future, it might even be possible for a loved one simply to upload all your texts, posts and online interactions with them to create an AI bot version or virtual simulation of you that they can talk to.

More and more people are using digital afterlife services. The ethics of this could be the subject of a whole book, but I'm mentioning it here because I want to shock you into the realization that every interaction you have online contributes to your undying digital footprint. Deleting won't work as there's usually a way to bring it back. Technology is always one step ahead. That's why it is super important that you delete or, if that's not possible, minimize most of your social media and messaging accounts right now. And when you do absolutely have to use them, do so on your own terms.

Quitting dependency on messaging apps and social media is essential for a strong mindset and a happier life.[21] This power move, which builds on the "stay away from your phone for the first 30 minutes of your day and go for a silent walk later in the day" foundations laid down in Power Moves 2 and 13, will help you take back the power you've given to your smartphone and return that power back where it belongs – with you. It will offer a motivational framework to help you stay as unplugged and as far away from dependency on social media as possible. It will encourage you to "like" less and live more; and every time you get the urge to check your social media unnecessarily, it'll inspire you to lift your chin, look up and learn something new instead.

Digital Eternity

Nearly everyone has a smartphone, often with smart speakers, these days. Every day of our lives, we're busy tracking ourselves, interacting online, sending status updates and receiving feedback, most of which is engineered by algorithms that feed on the data we provide them with. Those algorithms often know our lives and routines better than we know them ourselves, down to the videos we watch, how long we take to process information, where we are, who we connect to in person and online, what our interests are and even what our facial expressions and tone of voice are communicating.

All this information about us can be used to manipulate us in subtle ways. Even if you are aware of this and attempt to resist it, you may not fully realize just how subtly the online world can influence your behaviour, your mood and your perspective. It is well documented that social media use contributes to anxiety and depression and can destroy originality, creativity and capacity for empathy.[22]

If you're like most people these days, you probably use social media or texting apps and messaging for either your work or your personal life. And all this messaging can become addictive – and when a text alert, message, email or update arrives, you can't resist dropping everything to instantly check it. The lure of online interaction isn't in your head. It is down to two chemicals in your brain that are released every time you post or receive a virtual post, message or update. These two chemicals are dopamine and oxytocin. Dopamine is a pleasure chemical that's released when we want something, while oxytocin is known as the "cuddle" or feel-good hormone that's released when we fall in love, for example. That is why an incoming text, tweet or email has such an irresistible draw, with one study showing it's as addictive as nicotine and alcohol.[23] People also feel better about themselves when others react positively to what they post on social media. The "like" or thumbs-up button is a powerful psychological tool.

As well as your reactions to your news feed, think about how much of your creativity, time and energy are devoted to creating an online avatar, which in most cases does not reflect the real you – only the sunny or forced highlights. It is a façade designed to impress others. Time to impress yourself now and pour all that creativity, time and energy into living your real life instead, creating a photo album of memories in your mind.

One of the consistently popular social media memes are those that feature cats and their adorable antics. This is the ultimate irony as the most popular pets in the world are dogs. We love cats for their unpredictability and ability to make up their own minds. However, social media accounts are programming you to become obedient like a dog and not independent and free-spirited like a cat. Power Move Number 19 will empower you to have the absolute certainty and self-assuredness of a cat both when you are on and offline. It will encourage you to stop handing your personal power over to your phone and all those energy- and personality-draining apps. It will help you take back your power and come back to your own life in every sense. To yourself. To your creativity. To a social-media free life that's less dependent on the approval of others and way more interesting.

Acting Out: Case Study

Jo was thrilled when she was invited to become a cookery writer for a national newspaper, based on the recipes she posted on her blog about food. But a week before her first feature was published someone stole her online identity and Instagram shut down her account.

Eventually her account was restored, but it took nearly two months. During those months, her friends encouraged her to switch to TikTok, but she just couldn't summon up the energy.

She started to relish the silence and the free time she now had without having to pour so much energy into endless content creation and into analysing why one post worked yet another didn't, while never really knowing why.

She suddenly realized how much more at peace she felt, and how draining it had been to constantly perform for the camera rather than doing what she loved, which was cooking and writing about it. Indeed, during those two months she had a wave of creativity and created a book proposal about the joys of hearty soup recipes, which was then picked up by a literary agent.

When her Instagram account was restored, she made the decision to stay away. Being blocked was the best thing that could have happened to her, she felt, as she wouldn't have put together her book proposal without that incentive. Nevertheless, her agent was keen for her to get back online, saying it would increase the chances of Jo's book being taken on by a publisher.

Jo felt so much happier with her life, so she was prepared to take the risk of not getting her book commissioned. Nothing was more important than her well-being and she always had the option to self-publish, given that her profile as a cookery writer was growing strong.

Her friends were amazed and kept asking her why she was offline. When I asked her about it, she told me that she felt more alive offline and that she now had more time for the people, pets and things she really cared about. She also liked the sense of focus and not feeling compelled to reach for her phone anytime she had a break in her day. Instead of thinking how she can fill her time, she now thinks about what she can do with her time. And then she goes and does it.

TAKE ACTION NOW

Decades ago, excessive TV watching was believed to be damaging children's creativity. There was even a TV show in the 1970s that was ironically called *Why Don't You Switch*

Off the Television and Go and Do Something Less Boring Instead?. And that is exactly right. Interesting people are people who live their lives, rather than watching it unfold on screens.

Excessive social media and phone use has, of course, replaced watching TV as the boring choice today. There are positives to social media use – connecting us to loved ones, keeping us informed and educated – and it may not be possible or even advisable for you to delete your accounts entirely. It is essential, though, that you become aware of your digital footprint and the impact the online world is having on your creativity, originality, happiness, sense of self-worth and ability to feel in control of your life. Giving up social media, and/or becoming aware of and regulating your use of it, will open up your life. It will make you feel happier, lighter and more productive. It will make you more interesting!

- Before you tackle your social media use, from now on, every time you get the urge to check your phone I'd like you to just notice it, but don't act on it. Instead, I want you to lift your chin and look up at the sky or above your usual eye line instead. When we're not staring at screens, most of us keep our gaze level or look down at the floor. We don't notice the sky or what's happening above our heads. Even if you only see a ceiling, there's always something new to notice if you look up and take in a new perspective.

- If you find it hard to resist the call of your phone, don't beat yourself up. This is only natural, as you've been at the mercy of your digital device for a while now. Take small steps. Besides looking up at the sky or whatever is overhead, try listening to your favourite piece of music, or go for a brisk walk or write in your journal.

Do something life-affirming and non-virtual instead. Tell yourself that you will check your phone on the hour or at a set time. You don't have to check it right now. Even if you only manage to resist checking it for five or so minutes, congratulate yourself. You are starting to cut the digital ties that bind.

- At some point this week, you will need to review which social media apps you are on. If it's impossible for personal and professional reasons to delete them all, see if you can limit them to just one, or not more than three. If you feel nervous about deleting any of your accounts, ask yourself if you want to have a real life or a social-media defined life. Do you want to have an empowered or a life dependent on online feedback from others? Assuming it's the former, delete those accounts now.

- Of course you can't cut yourself off entirely from your smartphone, but you can ensure that you and not your accounts are in the driver's seat of your life. This is especially important if your work replies on social media. Becoming aware of the addictive quality of social media, texting apps and that "like" button is the first and most important step. Once you are aware of this, social media can then complement your life, rather than dictate it. You are the one in control here. So take action.

- Silence those alerts and set aside a time to review them when it's convenient for you. Most alerts are not urgent – even though the designers use manipulative tricks to make you feel you can't live without them. But you really can. Remember, these apps and platforms are businesses that need users. It truly isn't essential to see that funny cat meme right now!

- People with healthy self-esteem and a sense of purpose in life don't have their responses or moods dictated by the whims of a "like" button. Your self-esteem and what you're doing with your life matter far more than anything on apps and social media. From now on, loosen the addictive hold of that "like" button. When you post anything, do so because it matters or reveals the honest, authentic you. Posting simply to chase likes or FOMO is totally meaningless. And if you post something about yourself and nobody likes it, it really doesn't matter. Think about it – when a post about a psychic goldfish gets more "likes" than a profound quote by Ghandi, why does it matter how many "likes" you get? If your heart gives your post the thumbs-up, that's all the validation you need.

- And do take a good, long look at your profile picture. If you feel your photo captures your essence and presents you in an honest and positive light, that's fine. But if you feel it could be misunderstood, do yourself a big favour and change it. There's a whole emerging science of advice online about creating an appealing profile picture: it seems that a laughing smile showing teeth and slightly scrunched eyes (avoid hats or sunglasses), and a head-and-shoulders shot with a bright background works best. For women, looking directly at the camera is considered most genuine, whereas for men the preference is looking slightly away. Photos that look natural and believable are always viewed most positively. You don't have to look like a supermodel or an Instagram influencer, but you do need to look like someone who is authentic, helpful and engaging. And do update your profile every few years as well, as people want to know what you look like now, not 15 years ago. Constantly changing your profile picture can be just as disorientating, so find a happy medium.

- Remember, in the online world, when it comes to forging meaningful personal connections, truth and authenticity count more than spin, though it can often appear otherwise. Apply that same integrity and authenticity filter to your online friends and followers. Unfriend and unfollow whatever or whoever doesn't feel real.

- The next time something special happens in your life, stay strong and resist the urge to create a post or video online about it. If you visit a concert, rather than worrying about capturing that perfect image or video so you can share it online later, put your darn phone away and enjoy the concert in person, rather than through a lens. Create a lasting memory in your mind that you can return to time and time again, rather than your overpopulated online photo album. Be honest now – of all the thousands of photos and videos there, how many of them do you return to? Your phone and the insatiable demands of always being social media ready are stopping you living life as it should be lived – to the full in the moment.

- Finally, before you text, message, email, post, like, share or seek out online information or join online groups etc., make it a habit to ask yourself if you would behave the same way if you encountered or interacted with these individuals or groups in real life. Be the positive and compassionate change you want to see in the online world.

It seems obvious to say that politeness, integrity and kindness are just as important online as they are in real life, but the truth is that many people think of the internet as a place of escapism and fantasy. It's as if what happens there isn't real or isn't to be taken seriously, so they can comment and remain anonymous. But the internet is real in a sense. What we say and do there virtually matters greatly. Indeed, as mentioned at the start of this power move, it could be argued that it matters just as much as what you do in your daily real life, because once you make a statement online, in most cases it's recorded for all eternity. Even if you delete it, there's a chance that somebody else has kept a record of it.

With the awareness that whatever you say or do online will echo throughout eternity, make sure it's as positive, truthful, authentic and life-affirming as possible. Look up from your screen every time your phone demands your energy. Aim higher.

POWER MOVE NUMBER 20: Grass Roots

Whether you're already a dedicated nature lover or not, restoring a sense of connection to nature – a connection that's your natural birth right – will improve your happiness, health and self-confidence, even if it is for just a few moments each day.

Centuries ago, we were born in natural settings. There was no other choice: we had to be in tune with nature and feel at one with it, because our survival depended on our ability to understand and read it. An ancient yearning for a deep connection to nature remains in our DNA, but is often marginalized by the fast pace of modern technology, materialism and urbanization. Losing our sense of connection to nature can be extremely damaging and creep up on us unawares. Sometimes the simplest way to cure feelings of stress, anxiety, fatigue or apathy is through the healing power of nature. And you can don't have to go on a forest retreat or hike in the mountains to get your nature fix. Power Move Number 20 will show you that nature deficiency can be cured in simple ways, starting with a pair of muddy feet.

Down to Earth

"Nature deficit disorder" is the term used to describe the poor mental and physical health resulting from a lack of interaction with nature.[24] It's an increasing cause for concern among health workers and believed to be especially harmful for children. Several studies show that depression, obesity, and other health conditions are connected to nature deficiency.[25] Although spending time in nature is not a miracle cure for these conditions, the more that people are able to experience and appreciate nature or green spaces, the happier and healthier they're likely to be.

The sense that nature has something important and wise to communicate to us, if only we take the time to connect to it, is ingrained in most of us. Whether you gaze in wonder at a glorious sunset, a rainbow, a shimmering lake, or simply admire the beauty of falling leaves you are being enchanted by the beauty of the earth. You are sensing the voice of nature, the language of the earth speaking to you.

Research has also shown that the awe we feel when we see natural beauty not only uplifts our mood but has a positive impact on our behaviour.[26] This is because whenever we feel awe we're more likely to be kind and generous to both ourselves and others. In a nutshell, if you spend time appreciating the natural world, you are playing a part in making yourself happier and the world a kinder place.

To restore your connection with nature, you should ideally immerse yourself in it as often as you can. If you live in a built-up area, rather than a natural setting or in the countryside, this isn't as easy to achieve – but it is still possible. Once you fully understand its benefits, nature will always find a way to reach you. It's possible to feel connected again to nature in both outdoor and indoor settings. You just need to find ways that work best for you. While Power Move Number 20 will suggest various ways to get back to nature, a deeply soothing, immediately accessible and highly recommended way to connect with the earth is through barefoot walking.

You probably ran around barefoot outside when you were a child, but when was the last time you felt grass or mud or sand under your feet as an adult? When we walk barefoot we can encounter the living energy of the earth. We absorb that energy through the soles of our feet, so it can then nourish our body, mind and soul.

Walking barefoot outside has been proven to be therapeutic. The scientific term for it is "earthing" and studies show it can boost energy, improve concentration and ease stress. One research project showed that walking barefoot on grass significantly decreased stress hormones, because it encourages the release of feel-good hormones.[27] Reflexologists say walking barefoot not only improves posture and balance, but acts like a mini workout for your foot muscles, and stimulates acupuncture points on your feet that are good for your eyesight.

Should you be thinking this all sounds rather "woo, woo" and meandering away from the highly practical, common-sense approach to personal empowerment taken by this action plan, remember the importance for your personal growth of keeping an open mind. Earthing also comes highly recommended by the likes of *Dragons' Den* star British entrepreneur Deborah Meaden. Whatever the weather, even if it's freezing or raining, in the morning Meaden will go outside barefoot and walk around her Somerset farm.[28] She says that there is something about touching the earth each day and having nothing between herself and the earth that she finds incredibly grounding.

Acting Out: Case Study

Tucker grew up in a deeply dysfunctional household, but he was fortunate enough to live near woodland. When things became too much and he felt overwhelmed by family arguments and tension, nothing could offer his teenage soul more respite than lying on his back while listening to the birds sing and watching the clouds fade into different shapes.

When he turned 18, Tucker left home and went to university in London to study engineering. Reluctant to return home during his vacations, he found work as a barista and got rented accommodation. He enjoyed the excitement and distraction of the city life and when he graduated he soon found a job working as an engineer. He loved his job and his new life. He had a whole new set of friends and a strong loving relationship with his partner, John. The two of them moved in together and before long were joined by the pitter-patter of tiny feet belonging to a dog that the two of them adored.

After six happy years living together, Tucker proposed to John, but much to Tucker's surprise John declined, saying that although he loved Tucker, he wasn't ready to settle down. Their relationship fell apart when John decided to make his dream of travelling a reality and moved out. Tucker was heartbroken. Without John, his busy city life felt empty and worthless. And to make the pain of his breakup feel even more acute, their beloved dog suddenly passed away.

With no family to help him deal with his feelings of abandonment and grief, Tucker started to work longer and longer hours. He was swiftly promoted but no matter how much acclaim he received professionally and no matter how much support his friends gave him, this didn't bring him the peace he craved.

One evening, as he was walking home from work, he couldn't help but notice how beautiful the sky looked. It was a stunning mixture of sunset reds and glowing golds. Mesmerized, he decided to find a spot in a park nearby where he could watch it, unobscured by buildings. He leaned against a tree beside a pond, listened to the sound of the water ruffled in the breeze and simply studied the sunset. A wave of emotion washed over him. Tears filled his eyes, and he realized that although he had felt incredibly sad and been close to tears many times these last few months, he had never actually properly cried about the loss of his relationship and his dog. And as he cried, he noticed a tiny sparrow hopping close to his feet and even though it seemed totally irrational, he felt it was a sign from his beloved dog from the afterlife.

After that night of a thousand tears, Tucker got a new lease of life. Nature had been his solace when he was growing up and he made a commitment to let nature back into his heart and his life again. Today, whenever his energy is low or he feels alone, he seeks out the beauty of flowers, leans against a tree, listens to the sounds of birds and watches a sunrise, sunset or starry night.

Every morning, when he wakes up, come rain or shine, he makes sure he walks barefoot in his garden to help him feel grounded and to soothe his soul. Nature speaks to him in ways that therapies and other self-help fixes cannot.

TAKE ACTION NOW

The universal truth is nature is good for you. It brings a sense of perspective and calm that you may struggle to find in other ways. Make sure you find ways each day to reconnect with nature.

- Practise some barefoot walking. Take a small towel. Go outside in your garden or find a patch of grass, soil or sand or any natural surface. (Be sure to check beforehand that there are no sharp stones or undesirable objects!) Take off your shoes and socks and walk for a few minutes on the ground. Notice how it feels to have this direct contact with the earth. If at any point you feel anxious or worried about what others might think, remind yourself of the scientifically proven benefits of earthing. When you have walked for a minute or so, wipe off any dirt or grass from your feet and put your shoes and socks back on. Return to your day knowing that you have taken the soothing energy of the earth through the soles of your feet with you.
- If the weather makes earthing impossible or you're concerned you might cut your feet or pick up infections, or you feel uncomfortable taking your shoes off, you could consider an earthing mat. Simply buy a mat or tray and fill it with fresh grass and mud and then take baby steps on it from side to side. If you have difficulty walking you can simply sit with your bare feet on the grass.

You could also treat yourself to a spot of barefoot walking or sitting on a sandy beach.

- If you want to learn more about earthing and some of its famous endorsers, there is a lot of information online. It is a wonderful therapy for anyone isolated from nature. However, if barefoot walking doesn't appeal to you or it's not possible for you, here are some other ways you can get your nature fix, which have similar healing properties:

  - **Gardening:** tending to plants, and getting your hands a little muddy in the process, has been shown to have similar health-boosting properties to earthing.[29]
  - **Forest bathing:** this is a fancy term for spending time in nature among trees, but you don't need to seek out a forest to do it. If you live near a park or woodland, find a tree to lean on, or even to hug for a few moments if you feel brave enough. As you touch or hold the tree, sense how alive and wise it is. Some experts believe that trees have the ability to communicate with each other.[30]
  - **Merge with water:** through water we are all connected to nature and the wholeness of life. Water is a healer, teacher and a mirror. What is it reflecting to you? Set aside time to visit a lake, pond, river or the sea and walk alongside it. Let the water dictate your pace.
  - **Bird watching:** this activity can take you right into the wild heart of nature from your kitchen window, if you hang a birdfeeder outside. It requires focused attention and the power of silence, so brings with it all the healing and calming benefits of being present and mindful.
  - **Animal interactions:** if you're fortunate enough to own a pet, treasure any time you can spend with them. There is no greater mood boost than the

unconditional love of a pet who's happy to see you, however you feel. Whether you own a pet or not, learning more about and interacting with animals in a respectful and kind manner is an obvious and immediate way to connect with nature.

— **Cloud watching:** spotting shapes in the clouds may have been something you did as a child, and it's a great way to reconnect with the creativity of your inner child and feel part of something greater than yourself. Star gazing and watching the sun rise and sunset can also inspire feelings of wonder and awe.

— **Moon watching:** start to become aware of the phases of the moon, and whether it's waxing, waning or full. Perhaps think of your relationship with the moon as a symbol of your relationship with yourself. The moon shines brightly in the darkness and doesn't ask anyone's permission to do so.

In summary, if you're lucky enough to live by a park, garden, wood, forest, lake, pond, river, seaside or natural space, take advantage of it and make sure you get out there and breathe in plenty of fresh air. But if that isn't possible because you live in a built-up area and can't easily travel to get your nature fix, you can still connect with nature in small but significant ways, such as cloud watching, star gazing, moon watching or by bringing flowers, pot plants, crystals, herbs and other natural features into your home. Open your windows and curtains and let the light in.

If all else fails, you can watch some nature videos or listen to nature sounds and imagine you're out there. While this isn't ideal, and you won't get the physical benefits of spending time outdoors, it can trick your brain into thinking you're getting closer to nature, and you will still experience the restorative and calming mental and emotional benefits.

POWER MOVE NUMBER 21: Give a F***

You simply can't live a great life if you're trapped in people pleasing and look to other people and things for your sense of validation. You need to get a firm sense of your own worth first. Others won't respect and value you if you don't respect and value yourself. Self-belief is a work in progress. It doesn't happen naturally for most of us and it's born from a winning combination of self-awareness and self-respect. That's why the previous 20 power moves have drilled down on practical things you can do every day to help you understand and take better care of yourself, so that feeling great becomes the norm and not the exception for you.

However, there will come a time when an unexpected shift happens in your personal growth. And this shift is an exciting sign that you're making genuine progress and walking in great footsteps. It's when you start wondering how all this hard work on yourself can be of benefit to others. You feel empowered enough to want to make a positive difference in the world. You intuitively understand that you're part of something bigger and it's not just about you.

In short, you start giving a f*** about the legacy you're going to leave behind.

You continue to prioritize your own well-being, of course, but the well-being of others and the planet you live on starts to matter just as much. That's why Power Move Number 21 takes the spotlight off you and shines it on what you can do to be of service to others. If you feel you still need more time to work on yourself first, please take it. There's no rush. Revisit and refresh all the previous 20 power moves and work on embodying them. Relax and trust that Power Move Number 21 will call your name when you're ready to embody it.

Just Do It

Instead of feeling drained or diminished by taking time out of our schedule to do something positive or healing for the collective good, research consistently shows that most of us will feel energized.[31] Giving a f*** is the mark of true greatness in a person and as you are reading this book, I'm assuming that is your endgame, too.

Volunteering your services for free or helping those who urgently need your spare funds, time or skills makes a real difference in shifting the world in the positive direction of compassion and connection. During the 2020 pandemic, volunteer response reached an all-time high, revealing the best of human nature. As the world resets, the hope is that we all continue to make volunteering or being of service to those less fortunate a constant theme.

Bear in mind that not only is being of service to others beneficial or potentially lifesaving to those you are helping, it's also good news for you. Studies indicate that it truly is better to give than receive.[32] Giving to others will give you a sense of deep meaning and purpose.

The volunteering world has moved with the times to fit any lifestyle or schedule. There are full-time, part-time, one-off, micro, skills-based, hands-on and remote opportunities, and many, many more ways to volunteer. While making a regular commitment is ideal, you don't have to donate huge amounts of time or even sign up for the long term. So, when you feel ready to answer the volunteer call, there are no excuses! Just do it.

Acting Out: Case Study

After weeks of training, Robert became a listening volunteer for the Samaritans. He admitted to me that he initially did it because he was seeking employment and thought it would be a great asset on his CV. At the start of his volunteering journey, he felt a little daunted because he was only in his mid-twenties, and wondered if he had enough life experience to help others. Nevertheless, he was encouraged by the fact that he'd passed the training and had been given the green light by his more experienced mentors.

Over time, he began to look forward to his weekly slots on the phones. The hardest part was maintaining an emotional distance and not intervening during times of crisis, as being a listening volunteer means exactly that – you simply listen. What he heard on the phones is, of course something he cannot divulge, and there were occasions when he felt powerless, but this was outweighed by those occasions when he felt that being at the end of the phone genuinely made a positive difference to desperate callers.

Volunteering was having a transformative impact on his own life too. He started to enjoy his work as an economist more, because he no longer relied on his job to give him a sense of purpose – volunteering gave his life meaning now.

After several months of being a listening volunteer, Robert wanted to dedicate more of his time to those things he felt were meaningful. He decided to change careers and become a social worker. As challenging as that job is, he has now been a social worker for over fifteen years and wouldn't have it any other way. Volunteering completely changed his life.

TAKE ACTION NOW

You can start volunteering in very simple ways: giving old clothes and possessions to charity, helping out in a soup kitchen, joining a helpline, offering your skills or knowledge to good causes online and in the real world, or simply by calling an elderly person to see if they need any help. It doesn't matter what you do, just reach out to see if you can be of service to those in need in some way.

- If you aren't sure how to get started, perhaps begin close to home. Do you have any vulnerable or elderly family members, neighbours or friends who you can help in any way? If you prefer to work remotely, there are plenty of opportunities to help charities or good causes online by either donating funds, mentoring or offering your skills and knowledge. Simply do an online search for "volunteer opportunities" to explore what could be a match for your skills and circumstances. You could also help to organize events, sell things or join in with sponsored activities to help raise funds for charities. You could mentor students. Nursing homes, hospitals, homeless shelters and hospices always need volunteers. There are lots volunteering possibilities out there, waiting for you to explore them, and, in the process, help make the world a more compassionate place.

- In addition to regular volunteer work, remember that kindness is contagious. Your act of service will inspire others to be kinder. If you've ever wanted to make a difference but felt that your life wasn't going in the right direction yet, simply being kinder to others is the perfect way to find purpose and ensure your life matters. Keep your eyes and your heart open and notice or find practical ways to help others every day and as often as possible from now on. Make random acts of kindness with no thought of personal gain your great way of life.

- One of the simplest random acts of kindness – especially if you haven't got time to spare for regular volunteering – is to share food. Millions of people all around the world simply don't have enough to eat. Whenever you go food shopping, and if your funds allow, get into the habit of buying one or two extra items. Collect them until you have a box full and then donate them to a food bank. Countless people rely on food banks for their survival. If you don't know where your local food bank is, many supermarkets now have collection points that accept donations.

- When giving items to a food bank, do ensure the contents are nutritious and, most important of all, non-perishable. Here are the items recommended as the ideal food bank donations by the Trussell Trust in the UK:

  - cereal
  - soup
  - pasta
  - rice
  - tinned tomatoes/pasta sauce
  - lentils, beans and pulses
  - tinned meat
  - tinned vegetables
  - tea/coffee
  - tinned fruit
  - biscuits
  - UHT milk
  - fruit juice

- Remember also that non-food items are also needed by food banks, such as: deodorant, toilet paper, shower gel, shaving gel, shampoo, soap, toothbrushes, toothpaste, hand wipes, laundry liquid detergent, laundry powder, washing-up liquid, feminine hygiene products, nappies, baby wipes and baby food (but not formula milk due to UNICEF regulations).

- You may also wish to organize a fundraising event for your local food bank or, better still, volunteer to help package and deliver food at a food bank. And remember the "giving through food" theme the next time you pass a homeless person who is begging for money in the street. Instead of throwing your spare change at them, see if you can use it to buy them a cup of tea or coffee and a sandwich instead.

- While sharing food is a great way to help others, if you need more suggestions (along with those given in Week 3), here are some other simple and caring everyday things you can do:

  — Smile and say hello to a stranger.
  — Spare your time for people who matter to you – time is the most precious gift you can give anyone.
  — Apologize if you are in the wrong.
  — The next time you encounter unkindness or find yourself caught in a heated argument, choose to retaliate with kindness rather than mirror back what is being thrown at you. This isn't about being a pushover or even turning the other cheek, it's about responding in the way that's most beneficial to you and the other person.
  — Offer help to someone who is bereaved or in crisis.
  — Encourage others to succeed and help themselves.
  — Help someone who is struggling with their luggage.
  — Be happy for someone else's success and congratulate them.
  — Leave a generous tip if you can.
  — Give up your seat on a busy bus, tube or train to someone who needs it more. Offer to take a photo for someone.
  — Choose patience when you feel tension rising in a queue.
  — Be polite to everyone you encounter.
  — Say please and thank you as often as you can.

- See the person behind the job or uniform.
- Stay open minded and respect opinions that are not your own.
- Leave unwanted books or magazines in waiting rooms or on public transport.
- Ask for, and accept help from others if you need it, because helping you can help others feel good about themselves.
- If your volunteering preference is to focus on the natural world rather than direct person-to-person contact, there are endless ways to help save the planet. Become a litter warrior, reduce your plastic (and carbon) footprint, volunteer in animal shelters, go vegan, eat organic produce, recycle, recycle, recycle, and plant a tree or three.

Remember that every act of kindness, however small, has the potential to create a ripple effect – and sometimes just one compassionate act can transform a person's life. In the wise words of Aesop, "The level of our success is limited only by our imagination and no act of kindness, however small, is ever wasted." Perform acts of kindness for others not because you want to impress them or expect a return, but because of the astonishing person you are becoming.

However you decide to be of service to others and/or this amazing earth, your underlying aim is to make being considerate your second nature and an intrinsic part of your everyday life. The more acts of caring for someone or something other than yourself that you carry out, the more that compassion will become your automatic response. And the more you'll become a great person who doesn't just talk about, but who actually embodies the positive change they want to see in the world.

YOUR WEEK THREE ACTION CHECKPOINTS

This week you have been discovering the life changing magic of solo walking, keeping your word, listening more than speaking, learning from your mistakes, setting boundaries, letting go of what drags you down, cutting back on phone use, barefoot walking and, last but by no means least, volunteering.

Oh, my! You are amazing. Reaching this point in the book is a huge achievement, because it means your life is fast becoming rich in power moves. I salute you. Please don't forget to congratulate yourself. Don't underestimate the potential for greatness you've unleashed by reaching the end of this third week and your final checkpoint. Whether you fully comprehend it or not, you are walking in the footsteps of your own greatness.

As with the previous two weeks, check off which power moves you've taken on board. Then, if you feel ready, press ahead with perhaps the most impactful power move of all, which will electrify your Week Four and radically rescript and define your action-packed adventure of a life, moving forward.

Power Move Number 13: Walk, No Talk
Go for a walk without your headphones.

Power Move Number 14: Reputation Matters
Keep your promises.

Power Move Number 15: The Ears Have It
Listen more, speak less.

Power Move Number 16: Fail Again
Mess up a lot.

Power Move Number 17: Line in the Sand
Discover the power of no.

Power Move Number 18: Get Rid
Declutter your life.

Power Move Number 19: Look Up
Switch off your phone and go do something
life-affirming instead.

Power Move Number 20: Grass Roots
Feel the earth beneath your feet.

Power Move Number 21: Give a F***
Help others as much as you help yourself.

WEEK FOUR: DO NOT DISTURB

Time in your amazing company has flown by so fast! I can't believe we're already in Week Four. I'm going to miss you when our journey comes to an end, but I'm truly excited about the great life you're creating for yourself. There is only one power move for you to implement this week, but it is the commander-in-chief of all previous 21 power moves. It energizes and empowers all of them.

To paraphrase a truth expressed by the poet T S Eliot, what we typically think of as an ending is the place we start from. It means arriving back where we started, but understanding that place or that starter's mindset for the first time. Indeed, every day of our life is a chance to begin anew, refresh and reset, but most of us squander that opportunity with excuses and wishful thinking, rather than taking personal responsibility and acting.

All the previous power moves have in different ways helped you to grow in self-awareness and personal empowerment. They have encouraged you to become an admirable person of action, who walks your talk. Enact them in your life consistently and it will be impossible for you not to understand and embrace the crucial value of this supreme power move. It is both the beginning and endgame of all your personal growth. It is inevitable.

At the start of Week One of this action plan, you weren't ready to acknowledge the necessity of Power Move Number 22. It is the power move that will synergize all the others and which, day by day, each power move at a time, you have been gradually building toward.

In numerology, 22 is considered to be a master number, but whether you adhere to the philosophy of numerologists or not, Power Move Number 22 gets top billing. The other 21 are the essential supporting cast that have prepared you and paved the way for this turning point in your life. I have no doubt that you are ready for the defining Power Move Number 22 now, perhaps even be longing for it. If you want to change your life for the better, it must be implemented this week to ensure that your life becomes your great message to the world.

POWER MOVE NUMBER 22: Become a Ghost

The company we keep and what other think of us matters, but at the end of the day the only person who can decide and make your life a great one is you. If you've successfully been incorporating the previous power moves into your life, you'll be heading in the right direction and there can be no better time than now for you to learn how to disappear. Don't panic. You are finally ready for this. Power Move Number 22 is going to ask you to go into ghost mode, disappear, get off the radar, for as long as you need to.

Have you ever found that the only solution to a frozen computer or phone is to switch if off and on again? That is essentially what you're going to start doing more of from this point onward. You are going to go dark for a while each day to give yourself time to reset and restart.

Ghost mode is essential for personal growth. In the words of the inventor Thomas Edison, "The best thinking has been done in solitude." It involves seeking out time alone to reset and focus on your personal goal. This can be for a short period of time each day, or ideally a longer period stretching across several days or even weeks or months, but at some point – if you are to become all that you can be and to step into a better and stronger version of yourself – you must go dark. You must ghost everyone who has ever doubted you. You must create distance from the distractions, perspectives and expectations of others. You must know and fall in love with the power of being alone. You must go through the process of developing yourself and overcoming your limitations in the dark room, before you are ready to show yourself again. You must go off-grid and retreat.

You need to take time out to become more self-sufficient and resilient, so that when life's inevitable setbacks happen, you won't derailed by them. You'll learn from them instead, pick yourself up and correct your course.

The only way to become truly resilient is to step back, and know how to empower yourself in silence. Only in solitude can you observe yourself objectively and then successfully rewire your brain and force yourself to act. It is when you're alone that you realize you must only answer to yourself. Only in solitude can you become a self-starter. Only in solitude can you discover the wisdom to let go of what no longer serves you and open yourself up to positive change.

Silent Treatment

We are often told of the benefits of relationships and social interaction to our well-being, but an emerging body of research suggests that the ability to be comfortable alone can be both beneficial and life-enhancing.[1] The power of solitude is highly underrated. The studies show that people who enjoy their own company and are therefore not dependent on others for motivation or happiness have higher levels of focus, creativity and confidence. They also cope better with setbacks, because they know that they're the source of their own happiness, and it's their response, not what happens to them, that defines their character and directs their lives.

For centuries, solitude has been linked to creativity, empowerment and eureka moments in the lives of artists and innovators. Your mind is sharper and keener in solitude, and originality, and a strong sense of yourself thrives when it is free from the corruption of outside influences. In the words of the engineer Nikola Tesla, "Be alone – that is the secret of invention, be alone, that is where ideas are born."

Some of the most brilliant ideas happen in solitude, yet despite this, solitude still gets a bad press and is often associated with deprivation and loneliness. The fact is, in moderation, solitude is crucial for understanding who you are, what you want and for having a clear sense of self. Just as healthy eating, exercise and quality sleep are good for your well-being, so is regular time alone – but make sure that time alone is spent without your phone. You might think you are alone when it's just you and your phone, but you're not. The entire world is accessible and demanding your attention through your phone, not to mention all your family, friends and other contacts.

Previous power moves have already made it abundantly clear that being at the mercy of phones, screens and social media all the time drains our energy, original and creativity. Power Move Number 22 is going to double down on that digital detox advice and amp it up a notch to include a people detox too. It will urge you to get comfortable with solitude. To become a ghost for however long you need.

Ghost mode isn't the same thing as using silence as a tool to punish, hurt or avoid people you aren't mature enough to be honest with. That kind of silent treatment is psychologically damaging and only used by people with low self-esteem. If someone in your life gives you the silent treatment without explanation, this is a serious red flag. Ghost mode is not about running away from difficult conversations or commitments. It is simply about choosing to take a step back every now and again from all distractions, noise and other people, so you can focus entirely on who you are and what you want, and strengthen yourself from the inside out and the outside in.

If you're thinking this is starting to sound a lot like the solo walking power move or unplugging power move mentioned earlier, you would be thinking along the right lines. Those moves have helped lay the foundation stones for this week's seminal power move.

Acting Out: Case Study

About ten years ago, I found myself pulled in a hundred different directions. As well as caring for my family and collaborating on a few projects, I was keen to help support newcomers get started in their writing career. Being a mature and modestly successful personal-growth author, I really felt I was ready to step into that mentor role. I was also incredibly grateful to have achieved some of my life goals – hitting the *Sunday Times* top 10 for example – and felt it was my time to give back. The wheels started to turn and before long I didn't have a moment's peace. My quiet writing life behind a computer transformed into endless meetings, beeping phones and events to attend.

Everything was very exciting and rewarding for a while, but then it wasn't. In my eagerness to collaborate with others, I over-shared and over-promised. Things didn't go as planned. Indecision on my part led to others making decisions I didn't endorse, not because they wanted to but because they had to. I lacked clear goals, vision and self-belief. I wasn't yet ready to collaborate or be an effective mentor. I needed to work on and mentor myself before I could effectively mentor others.

I let everyone know that I wished them well, but for my well-being I would be taking a step back and would no longer be available 24/7. Unless there was a strong personal connection, I cut off contact – and I didn't stop there. I deleted apps and social media that were distracting me from setting my own agenda. There was pushback at first and it wasn't always easy not to respond when people demanded something from me, but it really was a matter of sink or swim. It was the best decision I ever made, because once I went off-grid and stayed off it for several years, I rediscovered my intention and purpose. I understood as never before that seeking in others what I needed to discover in myself was not the answer.

After five or so years of becoming a ghost, I felt ready to emerge again. I had a clear vision of my publishing and media goals and a much-needed dose of self-belief. I also launched my own *White Shores* podcast without feeling the need to collaborate with anybody to do so. On the podcast, I could give a platform to newcomers and support other voices, but this time I would be able to do so from a position of clarity and strength, not confusion and weakness.

Today, I feel I am living my best life, but I still set aside regular ghost-mode time to recalibrate and reset. I give myself permission to hide away in my office, lock the door and enjoy the bliss of being alone. If I don't insist on that regular "me time" or alone time, I know I won't be able to function at my peak.

TAKE ACTION NOW

Over the next 30 days or more, make sure you get off-grid for however long you need to recalibrate and emerge stronger. Here's how to become a ghost in seven easy steps:

- **Step 1:** Going into ghost mode is about making time to be alone without distractions and to reset; it's not necessarily about disappearing entirely or going dark for days or weeks at a time. While in some cases, this may be possible and even desirable, if you have close family and other commitments, whether they be personal or professional, you can't simply vanish. You need to keep people who rely on you informed. You need to tell them that you are taking time out to work on your own goals and personal development. You should explain when and for how long you will be unavailable and how they can contact you if something urgent arises during your alone time.
- **Step 2:** If spending an extended period of time alone isn't possible, chose the optimum time every day to be entirely by yourself. It could be early in the morning

before everyone else gets up, just before you go to bed or a dedicated time you set aside each day. If being alone isn't possible in your household, then perhaps go for a walk outside by yourself, or hang a "do not disturb sign" on your door or wear earplugs. The important thing is this time is for you and for you alone and that you gift it to yourself regularly. Draw up a daily routine or block out periods when you can be alone and can focus on your vision and your personal goals.

- **Step 3:** Start with just 30 minutes of time away from everyone else with your phone switched off and build up from there. Free yourself from distractions both on- and offline and actively work on getting to know yourself. Be alone with your thoughts and give yourself an opportunity to observe them, rather than interact with them. This will help you understand that you are not your thoughts, or your feelings. You get to choose those thoughts and feelings. You can master your thoughts and control the narrative inside your head. Doing this will help you focus on what you can control in your life – which is your perspective and how you think about and react to things. It'll also help you acknowledge what is out of your control – and that is your past, what happens around you and the actions and opinions of others.

- **Step 4:** You can also use this time to define your goals, keep track of your progress toward them and adjust them if need be. If you've experienced a setback, instead of letting it crush and define you, use solitude as the perfect time in which to learn, grow and become a wiser and a better person because of it.

- **Step 5:** During your alone time, be sure to assess your holistic well-being objectively. Is your diet optimum? Are you getting regular daily exercise? Are you sleeping well? You are your own life coach, so if changes need to be made, this is your time to plan how to make them and follow through. You are a work-in-progress, constantly changing, so this is something you need to do daily.

- **Step 6:** It goes without saying that you can use your ghost-mode time to run through the previous 21 power moves in this book and monitor your progress with them. A sure-fire sign you're on track is that you enjoy solitude. It's your time to hold yourself accountable and to reinforce the idea that changing your life for the better is down to you. Paying for self-help seminars, courses or advice is simply part of delaying this inevitable accountability to yourself. Save yourself time and money – and gift yourself the power of solitude instead. The battle is always with yourself: the courage and wisdom you seek are within you, waiting to be discovered, but they can only be discovered when you get comfortable being alone. If you crave company or your phone in your alone time, notice this and write that craving down in a journal. Ask yourself if you want your life to be an endless scroll of newsfeeds and remind yourself of the vital importance of having a sense of self independent from your phone – not to mention the fact that the only person who should have control over your life is you and not the demands or opinions of others.

- **Step 7:** If you feel anxious or unhappy when by yourself – even if you spend just 10 minutes of time alone – that's only natural if you're used to being in company all the time. Just observe and write down those feelings, and be patient with yourself. Stick with it. Remember that solitude isn't the same as loneliness. The latter is a form of inner emptiness and lack, whereas the former is about choosing to be alone to work on your personal development and recalibrate. You can choose to have a full heart in an empty room.

When your ghost-mode time is up, be sure to carry the power of silent resilience it gifts you into the rest of your life. Get used to a little less conversation in your daily interactions. Consciously stop oversharing and explaining yourself to everyone. Keep your energy and power to yourself. You don't need to let other people know everything that's going on for you. Keep information sharing on a need-to-know basis. Show, don't tell, others who you are.

Focus without interruption on your own life and you will discover a quiet certainty about your own worth. Your brain and body are just waiting for you to give them the right commands. Say "no" to distractions and "yes" to the work you want to do. Then make or force yourself to do it. Your success is ultimately up to you. Quietly and behind the scenes take ownership of your own destiny.

Your mission now is to live a great life and be all that you can be. I hope you will choose to accept it. You may have to sacrifice parties and events, and to forego being "liked" or being thought of as a "nice" person by everyone when you become a ghost, but the journey of intentional self-improvement and the discipline, focus and commitment needed to undertake it, along with the courage to let go of what no longer serves you, must be discovered in the darkness – when it is just you and your brain alone together. Being comfortable alone is key to all your personal growth. Only when you are not dependent on externals for validation, treasure your own company and know your own mind (and can bear to be parted from your phone) will others know your value without you needing to utter a word.

In essence, never feel guilty about retreating yourself when you feel depleted. This is your sacred time to empower yourself from the inside out, so when you re-enter the world again you can walk your talk with even greater confidence, purpose and joy.

YOUR WEEK FOUR ACTION CHECKPOINT

Take time out alone to reset, review all the previous power moves and focus on your personal goals.

Power Move Number 22: Become a Ghost

Get off the radar when you need to and for as long as you need to.

CONCLUSION: ENDGAME

This is it. This is your endgame.

Everything you need to act out the life of your dreams is in place and you are ready to take centre stage now. There are no more takes or dress rehearsals. The stage is set. You have the knowledge. It is time now for lights, camera, action. The spotlights are laser-focused on you and what you're going to do with your precious life.

Are you going to let the 22 power moves define the rest of your life and help you make it the best it can be? Or are you going to carry on as before . . .? You know what you need to do now, because it's been outlined clearly for you here. But knowing won't get you to where you want to be. You must *do* what you know. You must act.

In the words of the industrialist Henry Ford, "If you always do what you have always done, you'll always get what you've always got." As you're reading this conclusion, I'm going to take your word for it and assume that you are already living outside your comfort zone and finding the discipline to assimilate the 22 power moves into your life. You are shifting your focus from contemplation of the knowledge, to scheduling time to act and then acting out that knowledge. You are making big changes in your daily routine.

Action Before Belief

What you believe is what you attract. What you think is what you become. But most important of all, what you do is who you are. It's your daily actions more than anything else that will create your reality and your reputation.

Choose those actions wisely.

This book will have made it clear to you – without a shadow of doubt – that the real secret is not to be found in affirmations, but in walking your talk. It is about acting before and/or alongside believing and then seeing. Moving forward, you can think of your action plan as a manifestation launch pad and augment it with as many affirmations as you like. But whether or not you choose to go in that direction, after working through this book, I trust that you will never again forget about the other seriously neglected half of the personal development equation: the power of positive doing.

Repeat after me:

The power lies not just in my intentions, but in my actions.

In other words, the defining magnetic force in this "like energy seeks like energy" world, is what you repeatedly do. The life-changing magic of your daily actions. What are you doing right now in this moment with your life?

Make an action adventure of your own life, starting today.

Ensure that the action of your life continues long after the four weeks are up, and the power moves become a natural part of your life – they effortlessly become something you just do. It makes no sense at all to stop after four weeks, because this is when you will really begin to experience the benefits. Don't stop. Don't look back.

Before I started writing this book, I already practised many of the power moves, but researching it and writing it down in this organized way has reaffirmed them all powerfully for me. I have all the personal proof I need that they work. However, my life is of no consequence to you. You need to find out for yourself. Stay on your active path toward personal transformation and nothing will be the same again, because from now on, you will know that your life will only improve when you understand that you are what you repeatedly do. You need to act and keep on taking action to attract the positive change you want in your life, rather than just dreaming about it.

At the beginning and end of your day, it is only through doing things, experiencing life, making mistakes, experimenting along the way, that the greatest adventure of all happens, and that epic adventure is learning. The only way to learn and grow is through the power of your daily actions. All that you need to know about the meaning of your life can be learned through what you repeatedly choose to do.

Right Back at You

I explained right at the start of this book how the meaning of the word "karma" refers to an action or deed that comes back to us – not a thought or a belief or even a feeling, but an action. So, take stock of your daily actions and consider what they say about you and what they are attracting back to you. Are you proud of the things you do?

And if some of the things you do don't work out as planned, or set you back or derail you, take heart. Remember what the previous power moves have taught you: that contrary to popular expectation, life isn't meant to be easy. This is so important it can't be repeated often enough. You learn and grow through endless challenge. The burned hand is the best teacher. Indeed, the research suggests that our brain gets more active when we're facing problems and challenges.[1] The next time you face a setback or disappointment, remind yourself that if you learn from it there is no failure. There is only evolving and becoming wiser. Every setback is a stepping stone to success. Every failure is an opportunity to learn how to get right back up again.

Sometimes growth hurts, but there is always light at the end of the tunnel. Like an alchemist transforms metal into gold, you can find within yourself the resilience to transform problems into purpose, rejection into resolve. And when you can rise above and see the bigger picture in this way, you'll become a walking inspiration to others, teaching them by your fine example.

Master Yourself

Working through the 22 power moves in this book and being consistent in your daily repetition of them – because the power lies in the repetition – will bring you to an inevitable conclusion. It's that you simply can't master the game of life or feel free and empowered until you master yourself. Mastering yourself involves being aware of your thoughts, feelings and beliefs and what they're creating and attracting into your life. It's also about becoming aware of how your actions – the things you do – define you, attract and create your reality.

Walk Your Talk has not just constantly reminded you of the importance of what you do, alongside what you think and feel, it has also hopefully helped you redefine your understanding of what success is. It doesn't matter how successful you are in the eyes of the world; unless you can master yourself first, you have nothing. You are but a "noisy gong and a clashing symbol" to quote 1 Corinthians, 13:1. Inner peace and power is the new definition of success. The 22 power moves in this book are dedicated to helping you become strong from both the outside in and the inside out so that, whatever happens in your life, you will always be living the best and greatest version of yourself. You will be a person of substance.

I'd like to mention Jim Carrey again here, who famously wrote himself a ten-million-dollar cheque before he became a global movie star. Carrey believes he manifested his dream of superstardom – he made it happen with the power of positive thinking – but even though he has lived a life most of us would consider wildly successful, toward the end of his life he has come to the profound understanding that none of that external success means a thing if you don't believe you are a person of substance.

Doers First

When I completed the first draft of this book, it didn't escape my attention that the movie *Gladiator II* was hitting the cinemas around the same time. I'd had absolutely no idea this sequel was in the works when I began writing six months earlier and referenced the great character of Maximus in the first *Gladiator* movie.

Only time will tell if the sequel matches the enduring appeal of its predecessor. Nevertheless, I can't help but love the synchronicity here, as the movie also features noble characters who show rather than tell others who they are.

Let's all reconnect to our inner gladiator and prove, rather than promise, to ourselves and others that we have the makings of true greatness. Let's consciously focus our energy on what we do and proactively become the change we want to see in the world. Visionaries will always have their place, but for the world to transform right now, we urgently need doers first – people like you who walk their talk.

Eye to Eye

If you've been reading a printed or digital version of this book, your eyes will have moved from side to side. And if you've been listening to it, you may want to move them from side to side now. There is some research to suggest that lateral eye movements stimulate both hemispheres of the brain – the logical and the creative – and improves connection between them.[2] This can enhance cognitive functions such as memory, focus and problem-solving. Additionally, these movements can boost dopamine production, which supports mental clarity, motivation and overall mood. So simply reading this book is priming your brain for greatness, but don't let all those good things stay trapped inside your head. You need to express them through action.

Whatever you do and however many setbacks you experience along the way, in the saying associated with the poet Robert Frost "life goes on", so always aim to keep moving forward. Life is much simpler than many of us think, when you consider that all you really have to make your mark on is the present moment. Gandalf, the wise wizard in *Lord of the Rings*, says this far better than I can when he encourages a frightened hobbit to rise to the challenge of his time: "All we have to decide is what to do with the time that is given to us." Notice again in this iconic quote, it is not what we decide to think or feel or dream, but what we decide to DO.

If you are living each moment earnestly and consciously walking your talk, you are already living a fulfilling life. You don't need to do everything today, but you do need to raise your expectations of yourself and do something that's in line with the best and greatest version of yourself every day. Your daily actions truly are the secret to your happiness and success.

If you talk about it, it is a wish. If you imagine it, it is possible. If you start doing it, it is real. At the end of their lives, people regret not what they did, but what they didn't do. Make sure the life changing advice in this book isn't something you regret not doing.

#DoSomething

"Action is eloquence." -
William Shakespeare, *Coriolanus*

NOTES

INTRODUCTION: SHOW, DON'T TELL

1   Y Shoda, W Mischel and P K Peake, "Predicting Adolescent Cognitive and Self-regulatory Competencies from Preschool Delay of Gratification: Identifying Diagnostic Conditions", *Developmental Psychology*, 1990, 26: 978–86.

2   M Norton, "The Research-Backed Benefits of Daily Rituals", *Harvard Business Review* website, 10 Apr 2024. Available at: https://hbr.org/2024/04/the-research-backed-benefits-of-daily-rituals

3   D T Neal, W Wood W, and A Drolet, "How do people adhere to goals when willpower is low? The profits (and pitfalls) of strong habits", *J Pers Soc Psychol*, Jun 2013, 104(6): 959–75. doi: 10.1037/a0032626. PMID: 23730907.

4   F Gino and M Norton, "Why Rituals Work", *Scientific American* website, 14 May, 2023. Available at: www.scientificamerican.com/article/why-rituals-work/

5   N M Hobson, B Bonk D and M Inzlicht, "Rituals Decrease the Neural Response to Performance failure", *Peer J.*, 30 May 2017; 5:e3363. doi: 10.7717/peerj.3363. PMID: 28584707; PMCID: PMC5452956.

6   A Wood Brooks et al, "Don't Stop Believing: Rituals improve performance by decreasing anxiety", *Organizational Behavior and Human Decision Processes*, November 2016, 137(4): 71–85. Available at: www.researchgate.net/publication/306422100_Don't_stop_believing_Rituals_improve_performance_by_decreasing_anxiety

7   R E O'Hara, "Using the Power of Ritual to Reduce
     Anxiety", *Psychology Today* website, 28 Oct 2024.
     Available at: www.psychologytoday.com/intl/blog/
     nudging-ahead/202410/using-the-power-of-ritual-to-
     reduce-anxiety
8   C A Hartley and E A Phelps, "Anxiety and decision-
     making", *Biol Psychiatry*, Jul 2012;72(2): 113–8. doi:
     10.1016/j.biopsych.2011.12.027. Epub 10 Feb 2012. PMID:
     22325982; PMCID: PMC3864559.
9   R F Bruner, "Repetition is the First Principle of All
     Learning", 28 April, 2020. Available at:
     www.researchgate.net/publication/228318502_
     Repetition_is_the_First_Principle_of_All_Learning
10   Jocelyn Solis-Moreira, "How Long Does It Really Take to
     Form a Habit?", *Scientific American* website, 24 Jan 2024.
     Available at: www.scientificamerican.com/article/how-
     long-does-it-really-take-to-form-a-habit/
11   From *Batman Begins* (2005), directed by Christopher
     Nolan and written by Nolan and David S Goyer.

WEEK ONE : YOUR TIME TO WAKE UP!

1   P McNamara, et al, "Impact of REM Sleep on Distortions
     of Self-concept, Mood and Memory in Depressed/
     Anxious Participants", *J Affect Disord.*, 2010; 122(3):198-
     207. Epub 24 Jul 2009.
2   Alice Berry, "Waking Up to Your Phone Alarm? It Could
     Be Putting You at Risk", UVA Today website, 19 Dec
     2023. Available at: https://news.virginia.edu/content/
     waking-your-phone-alarm-it-could-be-putting-you-risk
3   J Y Heo et al, "Effects of Smartphone Use with and
     without Blue Light at Night in Healthy Adults: A
     Randomized, Double-blind, Cross-over, Placebo-
     controlled Comparison", *J Psychiatr Res*, Apr 2017; 87:
     61–70. Epub 12 Dec 2016.
4   C Chen et al., "The Relationship between Self-esteem
     and Mobile Phone Addiction among College Students:

The chain Mediating Effects of Social Avoidance and Peer Relationships", *Front Psychol.*, 2023; 14:1137220.

5 Cleveland Clinic staff writer, "Should You Be Keeping a Dream Journal?", Cleveland Clinic website, 21 May 2024. Available at: https://health.clevelandclinic.org/dream-journal

6 Eric W Dolan, "Heightened Dream Recall Ability Linked to Increased Creativity and Functional Brain Connectivity", PsyPost website, 14 May 2022. Available at: www.psypost.org/heightened-dream-recall-ability-linked-to-increased-creativity-and-functional-brain-connectivity/

7 D Dal Sacco, "Dream Recall Frequency and Psychosomatics", *Acta Biomed.*, 11 May 2022; 93(2): e2022046.

8 M Schredle et al, "Voice-recorded vs. Written Dream Reports: A Research Note", *International Journal of Dream Research*, 2019; 12(1), 138–140.

9 Ibid.

10 Chris Weller, "A Harvard Psychologist Says This is the First Thing You Should Do When You Wake Up", Business Insider website, 30 Sept 2016. Available at: www.businessinsider.com/amy-cuddy-advice-waking-up-right-2016-1

11 Ibid.

12 iSkip website home page. Available at: https://iskip.com/about-iskip/

13 G Trivedi et al, "Humming (Simple Bhramari Pranayama) as a Stress Buster: A Holter-Based Study to Analyze Heart Rate Variability (HRV) Parameters During Bhramari, Physical Activity, Emotional Stress, and Sleep", *Cureus*, 13 Apr 2023;15(4):e37527.

14 Joe Leech, "7 Science-Based Health Benefits of Drinking Enough Water", Healthline website, 8 Mar 2023. Available at: www.healthline.com/nutrition/7-health-benefits-of-water

15 Theresa Cheung, *The Lemon Juice Diet*, Griffin Books, 2008.

16 Helen West, "6 Evidence-Based Health Benefits of Lemons", Healthline website, 16 Oct 2024. Available at: www.healthline.com/nutrition/6-lemon-health-benefits#the-bottom-line

17 A Yankouskaya et al, "Short-Term Head-Out Whole-Body Cold-Water Immersion Facilitates Positive Affect and Increases Interaction between Large-Scale Brain Networks", *Biology* (Basel), 2023;12(2):211.

18 G A Buijze et al, "The Effect of Cold Showering on Health and Work: A Randomized Controlled Trial", *PLoS One*, 2016; 11(9):e0161749. doi: 10.1371/journal.pone.0161749. Erratum in: PLoS One. Aug 2018 2; 13(8):e0201978.

19 A Yankouskaya et al.

20 K Johnson, S J Lennon and N Rudd, "Dress, Body and Self: Research in the Social Psychology of Dress", *Fashion and Textiles*, 2014; 1:20.

21 Dennis Green, "Dressing for Success Actually Works", Business Insider website, 27 Feb 2016. Available at: www.businessinsider.com/dressing-for-success-actually-works-2016-2

22 S T Azeemi and S M Raza, "A Critical Analysis of Chromotherapy and its Scientific Evolution", *Evid Based Complement Alternat Med.*, Dec 2005; 2(4): 481–8.

23 ABC News staff writer, "Eau de Pumpkin: For Men Pumpkin Is a Real Turn-On", 23 Nov 2010. Available at: https://abcnews.go.com/Health/MindMoodResourceCenter/sexually-arousing-smells-pumpkin/story?id=12226715

24 Ł Jach, M Moroń and P K Jonason, "Men's Facial Hair Preferences Reflect Facial Hair Impression Management Functions Across Contexts and Men Know It", *Arch Sex Behav*. Aug 2023; 52(6): 2465–73. Epub 17 Apr 2023.

25 V A De Menezes et al, "Prevalence and Factors Related to Mouth Breathing in School Children at the Santo Amaro Project-Recife, 2005", *Braz J Otorhinolaryngol*, May–Jun 2006; 72(3):394–9.

26 Kirsten Nunez, "What Are the Advantages of Nose Breathing Vs. Mouth Breathing?", Healthline website, 1 Feb 2021. Available at: www.healthline.com/health/nose-breathing
27 APA staff writer, "What You Need to Know about Willpower: The Psychological Science of Self-control", APA website, 2012. Available at: www.apa.org/topics/personality/willpower
28 Lia Steakley, "The Science of Willpower", Scope blog, Stanford Medicine website, 29 Dec 2011. https://scopeblog.stanford.edu/2011/12/29/a-conversation-about-the-science-of-willpower/
29 Marianna Pogosyan, "Becoming Friends With Your Future Self", *Psychology Today* website, 24 Jul 2023. Available at: www.psychologytoday.com/gb/blog/between-cultures/202307/becoming-friends-with-your-future-self
30 The Institute for Love & Time (TiLT) home page. Available at: https://loveandtime.org/
31 J Mossbridge et al, "Smartphone Time Machine: Tech-Supported Improvements in Time Perspective and Wellbeing Measures", Frontiers in Psychology website, 3 Nov 2021. Available at: www.frontiersin.org/journals/psychology/articles/10.3389/fpsyg.2021.744209/full
32 TiLT, "The Expanded Human Potential Pilot Program: A Collaboration with Cook County Department of Corrections (Chicago), April to June 2022", n.d. Available at: https://loveandtime.org/expanded-human-potential-pilot-cc/
33 "The Hawethorne Effect" (related chapters and articles). Available at www.sciencedirect.com/topics/computer-science/hawthorne-effect

WEEK TWO: REST ASSURED

1 Louisa Richards, "How to Keep a Food Journal", Medical News Today website, 22 Sep 2023. Available at:

www.medicalnewstoday.com/articles/how-to-keep-a-food-journal

2   W E Barrington and E White, "Mortality Outcomes Associated with Intake of Fast-food Items and Sugar-sweetened Drinks among Older Adults in the Vitamins and Lifestyle (VITAL) Study", *Public Health Nutrition*, 2016; 19(18): 3319–26.

3   B D Horne, "Considerations for the Optimal Timing, Duration, Frequency, and Length of an Intermittent Fasting Regimen for Health Improvement", *Nutrients*, 25 Aug 2020;12(9):2567.

4   Alyssa Hui-Anderson, "Sad Girl Playlists Aren't Just Trendy—Study Finds Sad Music Can Boost Your Mental Health", Health website, 19 May 2024. Available at: www.health.com/sad-music-can-boost-mental-health-7504004

5   T Zaatar et al, "The Transformative Power of Music: Insights into Neuroplasticity, Health, and Disease", *Brain Behav Immun Health*, 12 Dec 2023; 35:100716.

6   John Stansfield and Louise Bunce, "The Relationship Between Empathy and Reading Fiction: Separate Roles for Cognitive and Affective Components", *EFPSA*, 2014; 5(3): 9–18. Available at: https://jeps.efpsa.org/articles/10.5334/jeps.ca

7   A Einstein, *Cosmic Religion and Other Opinions and Aphorisms* (Mineola: Dover Publications, 2009), p.97.

8   Nadine Gaab, "Reading and the Brain", Harvard Medical School website, Summer 2016. Available at: https://hms.harvard.edu/news-events/publications-archive/brain/reading-brain

9   Staff writer, "Kingston University Student's Research into Fiction Habits and Personality Types Reveals Reading May Make Us Kinder", Kingston University website, 22 May 2017. Available at: www.kingston.ac.uk/news/article/1856/22-may-2017-

kingston-university-students-research-into-fiction-habits-and-personality-types-reveals-reading-may-make-us/

10 Jeremy Sutton, "5 Benefits of Journaling for Mental Health", PositivePsychology.com, 14 May 2018. Available at: https://positivepsychology.com/benefits-of-journaling/

11 "Goals Research Summary" PDF. Available at: www.dominican.edu/sites/default/files/2020-02/gailmatthews-harvard-goals-researchsummary.pdf

12 WebMD Editorial Contributors, Mental Health Benefits of Journaling, WebMD website, 25 Feb 2024. Available at: www.webmd.com/mental-health/mental-health-benefits-of-journaling

13 Caroline Davies, "Write Down Your Thoughts and Shred Them to Relieve Anger, Researchers Say", *Guardian* website, 9 Apr 2024. Available at: www.theguardian.com/society/2024/apr/09/write-down-your-thoughts-and-shred-them-to-relieve-anger-researchers-say

14 S T Lai and R E O'Carroll, "'The Three Good Things' – The Effects of Gratitude Practice on Wellbeing: A Randomised Controlled Trial", *Health Psychology Update*, 26(1). Available at: https://explore.bps.org.uk/content/bpshpu/26/1/10

15 Ibid.

Week Three: DAILY RE/ACTIONS

1 Mark Travers, "2 Ways The 'Silent Walking' Trend Can Supercharge Your Brain", *Forbes* website, 3 Nov 2023. Available at: www.forbes.com/sites/traversmark/2023/11/03/2-ways-the-silent-walking-trend-can-supercharge-your-brain/

2 A H Xiang et al, "Depression and Anxiety Among US Children and Young Adults", *JAMA Netw Open*, 2024; 7(10): e2436906.

3   K Mikkelsen et al, "Exercise and Mental Health",
     Maturitas, 2017; 106: 48–56, Available at: www.
     sciencedirect.com/science/article/pii/S0378512217308563

4   Lauren Suval, "Why Do We Care What Others Think?",
     PsychCentral website, 7 Feb 2012. Available at: https://
     psychcentral.com/blog/why-do-we-care-what-others-
     think#1

5   Leslie Becker-Phelps, "Why You Care What Others
     Think, and Why It's Not a Bad Thing", *Psychology Today*
     website, 7 Aug 2023. Available at:
     www.psychologytoday.com/gb/blog/making-
     change/202308/why-you-care-what-others-think-and-
     why-its-not-a-bad-thing

6   Jessica Wolf, "Is Kindness Contagious?", UCLA website,
     5 Jan 2023. Available at: https://newsroom.ucla.edu/
     magazine/bedari-kindness-institute-contagious

7   H Weger et al., "The Relative Effectiveness of Active
     Listening in Initial Interactions", *International Journal of
     Listening*, 2014; 28(1): 13–31.

8   L. Dossey, "The Helper's High", *Explore* (NY), 2018; 14(6):
     393–9.

9   P T Iorhen, "Listening Skills: A Tool for Effective
     Leadership", *International Journal of Management and
     Commerce Innovations*, 2019; 7(2): 584-594). Available at:
     www.researchpublish.com/upload/book/LISTENING%20
     SKILLS-8297.pdf

10   John Kluge, "Why the Road to Success Is Paved with
     Failure", *Forbes* website, 26 Feb 2014. Available at:
     www.forbes.com/sites/johnkluge/2014/02/26/why-the-
     road-to-success-is-paved-with-failure/

11   Bryan E Robinson, "Why Failure Is Your Ally",
     Psychology Today website, 18 Sep 2020. Available
     at: www.psychologytoday.com/gb/blog/the-right-
     mindset/202009/why-failure-is-your-ally

12   For safety guidance when wild swimming, visit the
     Royal National Lifeboat Institution (RNLI) website at

https://rnli.org/safety/choose-your-activity/open-water-swimming# and the Outdoor Swimming Society at www.outdoorswimmingsociety.com/is-it-safe/

13 Jay Vera Summer, "Napping: Benefits and Tips", Sleep Foundation website, 11 Mar 2024. Available at: www.sleepfoundation.org/napping.

14 Jo Nash, "How to Set Healthy Boundaries & Build Positive Relationships", PositivePsychology.com, 5 Jan 2018. Available at: https://positivepsychology.com/great-self-care-setting-healthy-boundaries/

15 Rich Oswald, "Map It Out: Setting Boundaries for Your Well-being", *Speaking of Health* blog, Mayo Clinic Health System website, 27 Dec 2023. Available at: www.mayoclinichealthsystem.org/hometown-health/speaking-of-health/setting-boundaries-for-well-being

16 S I Kim, S Hwang and M Lee, "The Benefits of Negative Yet Informative Feedback", *PLoS One*. 19 Oct 2018; 13(10): e0205183.

17 See: Marie Kondo, *The-Life Changing Magic of Tidying: A Simple, Effective Way to Banish Clutter Forever* (London: Vermilion, 2014).

18 "Why Clutter Stresses Us Out, with Dn. Joseph Ferrari, PhD", *Speaking of Psychology* podcast, episode 227, APA website. Available at: www.apa.org/news/podcasts/speaking-of-psychology/clutter

19 Libby Sander, "What does Clutter do to Your Brain and Body?", NewsGP website, 25 Jan 2019. Available at: www1.racgp.org.au/newsgp/clinical/what-does-clutter-do-to-your-brain-and-body

20 C J Rogers and R Hart, "Home and the Extended-self: Exploring Associations between Clutter and Wellbeing", *Journal of Environmental Psychology*, 2021; vol 73. Available at: www.sciencedirect.com/science/article/abs/pii/S0272494421000062

21 L Y Lin et al. "Association between Social Media Use and Depression among U.S. Young Adults", *Depress Anxiety*, 2016; 33(4): 323–31. Epub 19 Jan 2016.

22 Jaron Lanior, *Ten Arguments for Deleting Your Social Media Accounts Now* (London: Vintage, 2019).

23 Jamie Waters, "Constant Craving: How Digital Media Turned Us All into Dopamine Addicts", *Guardian*, 22 Aug 2021. Available at: www.theguardian.com/global/2021/aug/22/how-digital-media-turned-us-all-into-dopamine-addicts-and-what-we-can-do-to-break-the-cycle

24 S L Warber et al, "Addressing 'Nature-Deficit Disorder': A Mixed Methods Pilot Study of Young Adults Attending a Wilderness Camp", *Evid Based Complement Alternat Med*, 2015; 2015:651827. Epub 16 Dec 2015.

25 Ibid.

26 M Monroy and D Keltner, "Awe as a Pathway to Mental and Physical Health", *Perspect Psychol Sci.*, Mar 2023; 18(2): 309–20. Epub 22 Aug 2022.

27 G Chevalier et al, "Earthing: Health Implications of Reconnecting the Human Body to the Earth's Surface Electrons", *J Environ Public Health*, 2012; 2012:291541. Epub 12 Jan 2012.

28 Jess Chaffey, "Deborah Meaden finds calm at her home in Somerset", *Somerset County Gazette*, 20 March 2020. Available at: www.somersetcountygazette.co.uk/news/18313850.deborah-meaden-finds-calm-home-somerset/

29 I Panțiru et al, "The Impact of Gardening on Well-being, Mental Health, and Quality of Life: an Umbrella review and meta-analysis", *Syst Rev*, 2024; 13: 45. Available at: https://systematicreviewsjournal.biomedcentral.com/articles/10.1186/s13643-024-02457-9

30 See Suzanne Simard, *Finding the Mother Tree: Uncovering the Wisdom and Intelligence of the Forest* (London: Penguin, 2022).

31 F Tabassum, J Mohan and P Smith, "Association of Volunteering with Mental Well-being: a Lifecourse Analysis of a National Population-based Longitudinal Study in the UK", *BMJ Open* website, 1 Sep 2016. Available at: https://bmjopen.bmj.com/content/6/8/e011327

32 B Nichol et al, "Exploring the Effects of Volunteering on the Social, Mental, and Physical Health and Well-being of Volunteers: An Umbrella Review", *Voluntas*, 4 May 2023; 1–32. Epub ahead of print.

WEEK FOUR : DO NOT DISTURB

1 Emma Young, "Seven Ways to Benefit from Solitude", *The Psychologist*, The British Psychological Society website, 12 Sep 2024. Available at: www.bps.org.uk/psychologist/seven-ways-benefit-solitude

CONCLUSION: ENDGAME

1 R D Raizada and R A Poldrack, "Challenge-driven Attention: Interacting Frontal and Brainstem Systems", *Front Hum Neurosci*, 28 Mar 2008; 1:3.

2 C Wang and G Yu, "Investigating the Relationship Between Eye Movement and Brain Wave Activity Using Video Games: Pilot Study", *JMIR Serious Games*. 13 Sep 2018; 6(3): e16.

ACKNOWLEDGEMENTS

Sincere gratitude to action-orientated entrepreneur Etan Ilfeld for being the inspiration behind this book, following my interview with him about the "power of doing" on my *White Shores* podcast in 2023. I would also sincerely like to thank Mark Gottlieb, my constantly insightful literary agent from the Trident Media Group, Ella Chappell, for being such a wise and encouraging editor. Gratitude also to Sue Lascelles for her illuminating Edit, Daniel Culver for doing such a great job at proof stage.

I'm indebted to everyone at Watkins publishing involved in the production, marketing and promotion of this book, most especially, Caroline Lambe and Hayley Moss. I could not be happier and feel more privileged to be given the opportunity to work once more with a publisher that has such a respected history and reputation in the world of personal and spiritual growth and development. I am also deeply grateful to my inspirational publicist, Gail Torr.

Heartfelt thanks to my family and my little soul dog, Arnie, for their love, patience and understanding as I dedicated my time and energy into writing this book. And last, but by no means least, a world of thanks to my adventurous and open-hearted readers. You are the catalyst and spirit of every book I write.

ABOUT THE AUTHOR

Theresa Cheung is a *Sunday Times* bestselling personal and spiritual growth author. She has a degree from King's College, Cambridge University, and is the author of numerous bestselling titles translated into 40 languages, including *The Dream Dictionary from A to Z* (HarperCollins, 2006) and *21 Rituals to Change Your Life* (Watkins).

Theresa works closely with scientists and psychologists and has contributed features about personal development to *Bustle, Vice, Cosmopolitan, Good Housekeeping, Red, Grazia, Heat, InStyle,* Yahoo, the *Daily Mail,* the *Daily Mirror, Glamour, I Newspaper* and many more. A popular returning dreams and personal growth and development guest on ITV's *This Morning,* she has also been interviewed on Coast-to-Coast AM, FOX 32, Great Day Louisiana, GAIA TV and on numerous podcasts and other media outlets, including GMTV, Channel 4 and BBC Radio.

You can follow Theresa via her @thetheresacheung Instagram and Facebook and X author pages, listen to her *White Shores* podcast which can be found on all podcast platforms and learn more about her work at www. theresacheung.com.

If you have any questions or power move stories to share, you can email her at angeltalk710@aol.com or via her website and social media pages.

'The way to get started is to quit talking and begin doing.' - Walt Disney